I'M NOT
MISSING
ANYTHING

I'M NOT MISSING ANYTHING

by
Brett Eastburn

To: Charlotte

Brett Eastburn
2011

10 9 8 7 6 5 4 3 2 1

ISBN 970-0-9833586-5-7

Library of Congress Control Number: 2011941406

Published by
Corby Books
A Division of Corby Publishing LP
P.O. Box 93
Notre Dame, Indiana 46556
(574) 784-3482
www.corbypublishing.com

Manufactured in the United States of America

PREFACE

Hi there.

Thanks for picking up a copy of my book. I hope you enjoy it.

I'm guessing you know part of my story already. If you've seen the title and my photo, you probably have figured out that I'm living with no arms or legs.

That's unusual. Believe me, from the looks I've received from complete strangers, I know how rare it is to see someone like me.

But being unusual doesn't entitle someone to write a book. If so, every tall person or short person, thin person or fat person, would have their life stories on the shelves.

And frankly, I wouldn't read any of those books. I'm not big on reading. I rarely grab a book expecting to spend a quiet hour or two. I've never been that kind of guy.

The reason I've written this book is that it gives me a chance to expand my mission. Over the past two decades, I've spoken to thousands of people about overcoming adversity. Maybe you've been in one of those audiences. If so, you know what I'm about. This book can give you additional insight into why I am the way I am and, maybe, how you can tackle some of the problems that you face.

But this book also is written for the millions who haven't seen me in person, on TV or in videos. A book can go places I'll never get to visit myself. If I can't get you to hear my voice, I hope you can read my words.

I want to give people hope. I want people to feel like there are no obstacles too big for them to overcome. I want them to realize that there are a handful of principles I use that have allowed me to achieve the dreams I've had. And if I'm able to do it without hands and feet, they should be able to go just as far, if not farther.

So thanks again for picking up this book.

There are some other people I need to thank, too.

God, my parents, and my loving wife Chrisa.

FOREWORD

"HI, I'M BRETT EASTBURN," said the young man in the wheelchair as he stuck out his right arm ... or stub.

There was nothing I could do but grab it. We shook. And then we both smiled—me more out of relief. That wasn't so bad.

I later realized what an honor it is to know Brett Eastburn, who has no legs and no arms but more heart than anyone I have ever met.

As you turn the pages of this book, you will get to know Brett, too. You will learn how he taught himself how to draw beautiful pictures, how he became an outstanding wrestler and how he found a way to inspire just about everyone within shouting distance of him.

You will also learn how comfortable Brett feels in his own skin. That, in turn, makes you feel comfortable, too. Not because his situation makes you feel any better about yourself but because you realize that there really aren't any limitations in life—for him ...or you.

While writing a series on Brett for the South Bend Tribune several years ago, I spent more than a few occasions with him and his wife Chrisa. I hung out with them at their house, visited his favorite hangout and joined him with his parents at his childhood home in North Liberty. Normal, ordinary places that had helped him form this normal, extraordinary young man.

During one afternoon together, he beat me in a game of pool and helped get a catsup bottle flowing for my sandwich. He also made me laugh so hard that tears flowed from my eyes.

Twice, I watched him wow a gymnasium full of teen-agers. During the course of his presentations, Brett went from a curiosity to rock-star status with his sense of humor, infectious enthusiasm and I-really-can-do-it demonstrations. He connects with people. They may forget his punchlines but they won't forget how he stood in front of them (often on top of a table to look them in the eye) and made them understand that in the ways that really count, he is no different than them.

OK, Brett may be a little different because he tries harder—sometimes a lot harder—to accomplish tasks. But, hopefully, his example shows others that they can dig a little deeper, too.

Brett Eastburn has become an outstanding

motivational speaker and all-around good guy despite having to overcome his share of problems as a youngster: dyslexia, bed-wetting, asthma and -- oh, yeah—he was born without arms and legs.

He still is a man in full.

Bill Moor

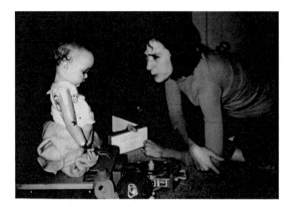

CHAPTER ONE

I USED TO CHEW MY NAILS.

It turned chronic. My Mom used to warn me that if you chew your nails it can hurt your cuticles. She forgot to say anything about my elbows.

That's how I open my comedy act. After I hop onstage on legs that have no feet, waving arms that have no hands, I use the joke to address the question that is on everyone's mind.

What on earth happened to Brett Eastburn?

The answer is, a lot of great things have happened to me. I've graduated from school. I've had a pretty impressive athletic career. I've become an artist. I drive

1

my own van. I've gotten married. I run my own business.

My stubs?

No, I didn't really chew off my nails, my hands or my feet. And no, I didn't lose my arms and legs in an accident. They weren't blown off in a war.

I was born this way. And it may surprise you that I thank God every day for making me the way I am.

I am different enough that people notice me wherever I go. Sometimes I might scare them or make them squeamish. They might stare at me, or they may try to ignore me.

But always, I make an impression on them. And I know, somewhere in their minds, they're wondering, what on earth happened to that guy?

I count on my unique appearance to catch people's attention. For the past couple of decades, I've given thousands of speeches to corporations, schools, military groups, church congregations and other groups. I have appeared on national TV and radio. A few examples are CNN, and The Bob and Tom Radio and TV Show. To date I have presented to and entertained audiences ranging from three to ten thousand people at one time—all together totaling to over one million people—in the US, Canada, Mexico, Japan, Aruba, and Switzerland.

My theme is "No Arms, No Legs, No Handicaps."

That's the message I've taken on the road ever since

my junior year in high school. That's when I decided I had the information and an attitude that I needed to share with others.

I travel over 200 days a year, performing "standup" comedy and speaking. I talk a lot at schools, but I am amazed most when I am able to change an adult's way of thinking.

I have a special reason why I like talking to business groups. I want business leaders to realize they don't have to be tricked or legislated into hiring people with disabilities.

Everywhere I go, business people tell me that their salvation will be innovation. They need to come up with better ways to produce different products to meet changes in the marketplace.

If you ever watch a blind person navigate through a lobby or see a guy like me throw a football, you'll never doubt our ability to innovate.

That's what we do best.

And I really enjoy the chance to meet children in their schools, especially the younger kids.

They not only listen but they have fun learning.

Elementary-and middle-school-age children find me interesting and funny. If I tell a corny joke or make a silly face, they laugh like crazy.

Another reason I like to meet young students is that they haven't yet learned to form preconceived ideas about people who look or act differently. They haven't learned to look away, to pity me or to hope I'll go away.

I've spent most of my life changing and perfecting my philosophies, which include learning how to turn handicaps into obstacles that can be overcome. This statement is sometimes viewed in the disabled community as offensive. But remember this: no matter how many times we change the meaning of a word or we label it with a different word, it doesn't change the situation I have been in for all of my life. The truth is I have a disability or a handicap and the important part is not to place it on others to try to remove it from your life. Sticks and Stones.

One story I've heard is about how the word "handicap" was formed. As the story goes, during the Crimean War a lot of soldiers were maimed in the fighting. During and after the war, it was common to see a veteran missing a limb being handy with his army cap to collect the extra change from someone who had been shopping in town.

Hence the word handi-cap.

I don't know if the story's true, but it's a good one to tell.

In my speeches, I often ask the audience to tell me what they think a handicap is. One time, a student way in the back was waving with both arms, really trying to get my attention. I tried to ignore him because I knew from experience, with the enthusiasm he was showing, that he had a doozy of a definition.

When my curiosity got the better of me, I called on him. He stood up and said, "A handicap is someone who is really messed up."

His friends all laughed. But his statement obviously is not true.

By the dictionary's definition, a handicap is not a person. It's a thing. More accurately, a handicap is something that will slow you down, get in your way or stop you completely.

So, in my opinion, based on that definition, I'm not handicapped.

Over the years, I've found only a few things that I can't do well. I've played basketball, football and baseball. I'm an accomplished swimmer. I was ranked fourth in the nation in my weight class in wrestling, I have studied martial arts and I can hold my own in pool.

I eat with a knife, fork, spoon or weapon of my choice. I have been driving legally since I was eighteen.

Sometimes I do things in slightly unconventional ways. But overall, things don't slow me down, get in my way or stop me completely.

Now that you know me a little, I should tell you about how I became me. It's quite a story.

I was born in 1971 in a hospital in South Bend, Indiana. As you might expect, my entrance into this world was a bit unusual.

Like a lot of young marrieds, my mom Barb and dad Vaughn wanted children. So they were thrilled when Mom got pregnant the first time. They were sad when the baby was miscarried, but Mom was pregnant again soon.

This second child, Shawn, she carried to the eighth month, but he died shortly after birth.

Dad was in the military in Hawaii at the time, so Shawn is buried in a military cemetery in Springfield, Illinois.

I've been to see Shawn's grave once. It's in a big field with row after row of white headstones. There are four empty plots available there where my mom, my dad, my sister and I can be buried, if we so choose. I doubt we will use them because it is too far for friends and family to visit.

Also, it gives me the heebie-jeebies to look at a section of ground that is waiting for me.

Obviously, when it was my turn to be born, something wasn't quite right. We haven't gone and put forth the effort of having DNA tests or anything like that. So we really aren't sure medically how I ended up the way I did.

My mother didn't take Thalidomide or anything

like that. The drug, prescribed by doctors in the late 1950s for nausea, a painkiller and sedative, was blamed for widespread birth defects, mainly in Germany. Some of the people older than me with deformed arms and legs have been called Thalidomide babies. These likely wouldn't be Americans, because the drug was never approved for use here.

Nowadays, doctors routinely perform ultrasounds on pregnant women. They can check the baby's gender, monitor the heartbeat and even count the fingers and toes.

Well, I was born in an earlier time. And if doctors had seen me as I am on their ultrasound monitors, what could they have done anyway?

Mom was suffering from hay fever during her pregnancy. Maybe that had something to do with it.

There's another theory we've done some checking into. There was a child born in Kentucky 30 years after me who has the exact same dimensions as me—a right arm that ends at the elbow, a left arm less than half that size and her legs are the same way as mine.

When we visited her, we spoke with her parents in detail, trying to figure out if there was anything that would link the two of us together.

The best connection we could come up with was that her parents and my parents both raised horses and chickens. Both families used a certain chemical to rub on their horses' skin. And chickens carry something called Newcastle B Virus, which causes chicks to be born without limbs.

These are just theories and have not been proven. But maybe that's it.

It probably makes no difference at this point. The most important thing that came out of that meeting in Kentucky was that the girl's parents saw how well I have tackled the challenges in front of me. If they had any misgivings about having this child, our visit changed their minds.

But getting back to the day of my birth, my parents were a bit more nervous than most would be. They already had lost two babies—one through miscarriage and another as a still-birth—and here I was being born two months prematurely.

After Mom's first contraction, she kept asking to be put under sedation for this delivery. The nurses said it would not be possible due to the dangers to her and the baby. After her second contraction, they placed a mask over her mouth and she sighed with relief and shouted, "Yes."

She didn't know it, but she wasn't feeling better because of a sedative. It turns out they were feeding her straight oxygen. The third contraction soon came and out popped little me.

Seconds after I was born, I was whisked out of the

room. Mom had her eyes shut tight because of her fear of blood and guts.

Still, Mom was scared. With her eyes tightly shut, she had asked a nurse, "What did I have?" And was told, "I didn't look at that." It was the same response she had received when Shawn was born.

Another nurse came back in, and Mom asked, "Is the baby alright?" The nurse broke down and started sobbing. This made Mom think that I was dead.

Person after person kept coming into the room to look at her and observe any emotional changes, and still no one would give her relief to the question, "Is the baby OK?"

The word soon spread through the hospital that Mom had a baby with no arms and legs. All sorts of people were staring at her through the windows. She felt like she was in a science-fiction movie, but she still didn't know why. At the same time these doctors and nurses were rushing in to see me. I was a celebrity already.

Years after I was born, Mom found out the details from a nurse who was there that day.

The doctor finally came in and said, "You have a baby boy. His heart's good. His lungs are good. But his extremities are not fully formed."

That final bit of information didn't seem so important to her. She only wanted to hear that I was alive.

9

The phrase "not fully formed" flew in one ear and out the other. Mom knew only that she finally had a baby she could take home. She knew she could love me.

Out in the waiting room my dad knew something had gone wrong with the delivery. He's always been a physical person—a hard worker, a handyman. He says it was a shock for him when he first saw me, without hands and feet.

Mom recalls how, when the doctors and nurses had cleared away, Dad came in with a face all droopy. He said, "This one's going to be a lot of work," and she said, "I don't care." And that, according to her, was the last time that they discussed it.

They might have nurses crying, doctors probing around trying to figure out where my fingers and toes were hiding, and friends showering them with pity, but in just minutes, they decided to accept me the way I am. Their lives truly were going to be "a lot of work," thanks to me. Because the sequence of events were so similar to when Shawn was born, they felt that this was the hand of God to help them accept me the way I was.

But you have to think—whatever I've accomplished in my life, whatever inspiration I've been able to give to others—none of that would have been possible if my parents had reacted differently than they did.

Soon after, St. Joseph Hospital closed its obstetrics department. Mom jokes that they probably had a hard time getting over me.

Over the years, people have said some really thoughtless things to her about me. Mom remembers one trip to a pediatrician's office when a little girl saw me and started to make a fuss. The mom just shushed her and said, "Just be glad you weren't born like that."

The mother said it loud enough that Mom and I both heard it. Thinking back, she says, she wished she had turned to me and said, "Just be glad that woman isn't your mother." There are so many things she could have said so many times, but she decided to just let the mean words go.

One of my favorite pictures is of my father holding me in one hand, all two pounds and eleven ounces of me, showing off his new baby boy.

And, as the story goes, he's saying to his friends, "Look what I made."

In his eyes, I was his perfect baby. I wasn't missing anything.

CHAPTER TWO

*"When you say, "I can't," you're right
because you're not even going to try."*
— Brett Eastburn

GO TO ANY BOOKSTORE these days and you'll see a lot of authors with ideas on how to raise babies.

The basic premise is: those early years are so important to a child's development. If you want your child to excel in a difficult world, you need to go beyond feeding, clothing and changing diapers.

Simple love and common sense aren't enough. Parents need a plan.

These books are popular because babies don't come with owner's manuals. When you take your firstborn home from the hospital, you might get a pinch of good advice from Grandma or a pediatrician, if you're lucky. But otherwise, you're on your own.

With that in mind, can you imagine how difficult it must have been for my parents back in 1971?

Beyond Dr. Spock, who sold more than 50 million books, and a handful of other experts, there wasn't a lot of good information out there. And how many experts would have had anything to say about raising a baby like me? As far as they knew, babies like me didn't exist.

I suppose the natural thing for a mom to do would be to try to keep Little Brett as happy as possible. Poor little baby needs this. Poor little baby needs that.

Maybe Mom should wait on me, pardon the expression, hand and foot. It would make perfect sense for her to run and help whenever I called.

That wasn't Mom's style.

One of the breakthrough stories I've heard from my parents involves my shirtsleeves. You've seen those cute baby outfits. For whatever reason, they all seemed to have long sleeves.

For babies with hands, that's not a problem. But for me, that meant a lot of sleeve just hanging in the wind at the ends of my stubs. So if someone tried to hand me a ball or a toy, it would just slide off those empty sleeves and roll away from me.

Basically, I would pick it up and drop it. Pick it up and drop it.

One day, my mom just decided to roll up the sleeves so my arms would poke through. That was the day she learned I could figure out how to hold onto something, as long as I was given a fair chance.

From there, it was a short step to realizing I could develop the skills and desire to be independent. Just because I didn't have hands, it didn't mean I wasn't using my brain or that I chose to be lazy.

But even though I had the power, it didn't mean I always was eager to do things for myself. I suppose I was like all babies. I wanted what I wanted when I wanted it. And when I heard the word "no," I was upset.

I thought I had the meanest parents ever. What kid doesn't?

Loyal Wilson, a family friend, tells of the time he was visiting the house when I was very little. I asked my mother to do something for me, but she said, "No, do it yourself."

Loyal recalls being a little angry with Mom. It seemed selfish and heartless for her to ignore my needs. It was years later, Loyal says, when he realized she knew exactly what she was doing. "Tough love," he calls it.

In my presentations, I include a segment on how my mother's willingness to let me try—and fail—helped me learn how to do the things I wanted to do.

There's a comic bit I use about the first time I tried to get out of a chair by myself. It resulted in a one-point landing—on my nose. But after several times of bruising my chin, I found out I could put my right arm down on the seat and pivot the rest of me out of the chair.

That was the first step on my way to see the rest of the world. If I had let the first bruise beat me, I never would have gotten to see Japan, Okinawa, Aruba, Switzerland or any of the other great places I've been.

Soon, I grew bolder and more inventive. I learned that a broomstick would help me open a refrigerator door. I learned that I could climb to the top of a kitchen counter if I opened cabinet drawers to create a personal staircase.

I learned I could put my chest in a Tonka dump truck and use my right arm and left leg to propel myself around the house.

It all came from my mom and dad having the courage to say, "No, do it yourself."

Early on, she started to see things about me that gave her hope. One day she saw me work and work with my stubs, trying to pick up a ribbon that had pulled loose from a toy. Another time, she heard a squeaking sound from the living room and found out I had crawled off the floor, up on a rocker.

A doctor connected her with a crippled children's group in Grand Rapids, Michigan. There, they made a bucket device she could put me into so I could sit up. Thank goodness for that. Before that, because I didn't have full legs, I couldn't balance myself to sit up on my own until I was 22 months old.

Without the bucket, I would have spent my first 22 months on my back, looking up at the ceiling. Not very interesting.

A majority of my life has been about fighting off boredom. That's what keeps me going. So even as an infant, I would get up and do stuff just to avoid boredom.

Maybe, in some ways, my mom and dad were lucky that I was the first baby they raised. They didn't have another baby to compare me with. There wasn't a lot of pressure to have me crawling or sitting up by a certain age.

Their idea for me would be good advice for anyone: There's something he's going to be good at. Let him blossom.

By the time I was school age, I had found a variety of ways to get myself from here to there. We lived in a small house, out in the country, and I could hop around on my butt to almost anywhere I wanted to go outdoors.

My great-grandmother bought me a skateboard—I still have it all these years later—that I used outdoors on the sidewalk. I could lie on it face down and push myself along, using my right arm and left leg.

For a while, I also had a little red motorized truck. I could lie on the seat on my stomach, steer with my little arm and push on the gas pedal with my big arm.

But my best method of transportation came when I finally met the boy who lived across the street from us. Jason Kaser was three or four years younger than me, but we became best buddies when he finally was old enough to cross the road and come play in my yard.

If he was bothered at all that I was different from him, he got over it quickly.

I may have changed his thinking one day when we were talking about sitting in my father's pickup truck. "How are you going to do that?" he asked. I asked him to open the driver's-side door. I quickly hopped up onto the truck floor and then hopped up into the seat. He never had to ask again.

He knew early on what I was about. If there was a problem, it might slow me down just a little, but I was going to find a way to deal with it. Kids move on

18

much faster than adults. With Jason as my playmate, a bigger world opened up to me.

We had a three-wheel vehicle that was called the Hot Seat. It was a thing of beauty with a chopper front end, a teardrop gas tank, a flared-out seat and extra-wide slick tires. To this day, I want to build a motorcycle like that trike.

I would climb aboard the Hot Seat and Jason would push me back into the farm fields and the woods. He eventually became a track star, and I'm guessing he built up his legs pushing that Hot Seat with me in it. I think I deserve half of his track trophies.

There are some places a Hot Seat couldn't go. If the field was muddy or if the grass was too high, the little wheels wouldn't turn. That's how we invented another method of transportation, which we called the Back Pack.

I would throw my arms around Jason's or another buddy's neck and ride on his back, just like Yoda did with Luke Skywalker in *Star Wars*. By the way, we were doing this before that movie came out.

Once I had my transportation figured out, all things considered, I had a typical farm-kid childhood. I was a Boy Scout, and I loved the outdoors. We explored, climbed trees, rode bikes and played in the dirt.

Eventually, other kids joined our little group. Another neighbor, David Brooke, and I were like brothers. We basically lived at each other's houses, and he's still one of my best friends, all these years later.

North Liberty is a small farming community, where all the kids know each other. We played all day long. It was like the Little Rascals, the kids you would see in the old movies back then. For as long as I can remember, I was in a group like that.

I never felt like a fringe player, either. People who know me from then still call me "The Fearless Leader," or "The Stub." I was the guy suggesting the adventures. If I could come up with an idea on something to do, I could find people willing to do it with me.

I wasn't the sort then to sit at a window and watch the world go by.

Years after I was born, my parents wanted another child. They decided to adopt a little girl but, before they finalized it, mom told me we were going to have a baby girl. I was about 5 years old, and I thought it would be fun to have a little sister. I was hopping up and down on the couch saying, "Oh good, she will have arms and legs just like me." Mom was a little stunned and said, "No, she will have arms and legs like me and Dad."

That's how Krista became part of the family. It was great to have someone I could play with and teach new things to.

I love being a big brother to someone who is taller than me. I remember going to Potato Creek with my perfectly formed little sister to catch crawdads. My father and grandfather had taught me to fish, and I figured we could use the crawdads for bait. We would wade out in the creek—chest high for me and knee high for Krista.

We caught 40 or so in a net and took them home. We had so much fun doing it that it didn't bother me too much when I found out that crawdads are not a good bait.

One of my happiest, earliest memories is of fishing in Potato Creek. I believe it taught me patience, but it also taught me a lot about fellowship. It's a way for friends and family to get together, tell stories and jokes, and basically enjoy each other's company while sitting in a boat. If you disagree with someone, you had to stay and work things out. There was no place else to go.

My Mom tells of a time when Dad took me ice fishing when I was really young. I was zipped into a snowmobile suit and spent most of the time hopping and sliding around on the ice. I was so wet and cold by the end of the day that I was turning blue, but I absolutely loved it.

That was the last time I went ice fishing with Dad. We came home half-frozen and with no fish. Mom was ready to kill Dad for that, or at least slap him.

When I was 15, my dad, both grandfathers and an uncle took me up to Geraldton, Ontario, for a full week of fishing. I ended up catching a northern pike that stretched nearly 3 feet. It was taller than I was. Biggest one of the trip!

These days, I still enjoy a good day of fishing, but only if the weather's perfect. My wife Chrisa likes fishing too, but she won't go if I insist on baiting my own hook. The way I learned to do it was to put the worm between my arm and my leg and put the hook in my mouth and pull the hook into the worm.

She says it grosses her out.

Another childhood memory is of getting into big trouble for setting a field on fire on the hottest day of the year. A friend and I were pretending to be firemen, so we would start fires and snuff them out with our shirts. Unfortunately, we waited a bit too long to start the snuffing. The breeze we created by waving our shirts simply caused the fire to spread.

We were so afraid to admit what we had done, we both wanted to run back home and not tell anyone. But we realized we would be in deeper trouble if the fire spread to the elementary school building at the edge of the field. I told my buddy to go tell our neighbor, who lived right by the school to get help.

The fire department came and put the fire out. As they were doing their job, I came around the corner, racing to the house saying, "I don't know why I did it, I don't know why I did it."

It's not one of those things I'm proud of, but I learned a lesson. If you want to take credit for your good works, you have to take responsibility for your mistakes. And admit what you've done before it becomes a real disaster.

Like a lot of kids, I saw my life change once my school years started.

For one, when I started kindergarten, I ended up with a motorized wheelchair. I didn't realize when I got one how much a wheelchair can be a huge part of your life. The wheelchair gave me independence to a higher level, but it also came with responsibilities I never had before.

There are all kinds of motorized chairs. They really are like a small golf cart. You can spend thousands of dollars on them and end up with options like front-wheel drive or zero-turn radius.

My first one wasn't one of those. It had two speeds, stop and go.

I had one chair that had the devil inside it. It would go through crazy spells and ram into tables. Teachers would blame me for it and tell me to stop trying so hard to get attention.

But then one day, with teachers watching, the chair started spinning wildly around, pitched me onto the floor, ran over one of my classmates and knocked over some desks. It was like a novel Stephen King should write, *The Psycho Wheelchair*.

I had also started school with artificial legs and arms. Doctors from the amputee clinic recommended this. However, the fake legs were a bad idea from the get-go. It was a horrid ordeal for me.

I had learned all these different ways to get around just fine. Now I had to strap on these nasty prosthetics that ended up causing a hernia and boils. I hated them.

Maybe that's when I got my real start as a persuasive speaker. I talked the school out of requiring me to walk on those legs. I do think that prosthetics are great for those who need them to replace a limb or for cosmetic reasons. I am grateful that I was made to use them. It gave me the choice to use them as an adult but they simply slowed me down. I am not missing anything, nothing was amputated, they felt like someone strapped on two extra sets of arms and legs. Imagine if you were made to wear extra arms and legs and you were born with two legs and two arms. Learning to walk and do things with an extra set of limbs would definitely slow you down.

There was some debate whether I would reach my potential at the town's public elementary. There was a special school about 15 miles from my home in South Bend where I could be "among my own kind."

I can see the logic. I needed some special types of instruction. Imagine, for example, being a public

24

school teacher trying to show a boy without hands how to write.

Sending me to the special school probably was a mistake, too. All I was learning were the basic motor skills and the 3 R's. By the time I was able to return to North Liberty, I had fallen far enough behind that I needed to repeat third grade.

I was humiliated. My classmates were moving on without me. I would never catch up with them. Even now, I feel like I should attend two different class reunions.

While all this was going on, I had this other problem that was ruining my self-esteem.

I was a bed-wetter. My doctor said there was no real physical reason for it, except maybe I was just sleeping too deeply. It's one of those things that carries a stigma and makes you feel ashamed of yourself.

I couldn't go to a sleepover without worrying about wetting my sleeping bag and everyone laughing. If you're a bed-wetter, or if you know one, you know what I mean. I was 14 years old when it finally stopped. I was embarrassed like any kid but this was one thing that definitely was not going to ruin my life.

I liked the social aspect of school. That's where my friends were, but I didn't like reading and I didn't like math.

Frankly, I wasn't the sort to do well in school anyway, at least not until high school. I hated homework. On top of that, I have three types of learning disabilities: *Dyslexia*—a language-based learning disability in which a person has trouble understanding written words. It may also be refered to as reading disability or reading disorder; *Dyscalculia*—a mathematical learning disability in which a person has a difficult time solving arithmetic problems and grasping math concepts; *Dysgraphia*—a writing disability in which a person finds it hard to form letters or write within a defined space. And no one knew it. I'm more of a visual guy. Take that good book and turn it into a movie. Then I'll do well on your quiz.

Later, when all my close friends were into cars, I would spend hours watching them wrench them up. I didn't have knuckles to skin under the hood, but from watching them, I pretty much can tell you how to take a car apart and put it back together.

By the end of my elementary years, I knew what I wanted to do with my life. I knew I had a message about overcoming obstacles that I could get out to people.

Maybe I would make a movie. But whatever it was, I wouldn't have to read, add or subtract to get it done.

I had my first real crisis during my seventh-grade year. It started when my motorized wheelchair broke down. I wasn't too alarmed at first, even though I was told it might take two or three months to fix.

I tried to get from class to class using my old skateboard. It wore me out. Then I tried to use a manual wheelchair, but because one arm is longer than the other, all I could do is roll myself in circles. I literally was going nowhere fast.

One solution was for my classmates to push me in the manual chair. It worked well at first. Whoever got the chance to push the chair got a sense of being a celebrity. But then the novelty wore off.

The school bell would ring and the kids would run out of the room, not looking back. No one wanted to push me.

So the teachers came up with a solution. They would assign a student each day to be my pusher.

This was one of those cases of unintended consequences. With this new system, I wasn't a friend anymore. I was an assignment. Most seventh-graders do not like assignments.

There was a second reason it didn't work. Every night, I was spending three or four hours on homework. Because I was dyslexic, it took me longer to read. Because I had no hands, it took me longer to write. Still, I did the work. But when it came time to turn it in, my papers and books often were in someone else's locker.

I ended up doing all that work but still getting zeroes on my homework.

There I was, going through the troubles of adolescence with this additional burden. My friends saw me as extra work so they didn't want to be around me. The teachers were unhappy because they thought I wasn't getting my work done. My parents were upset because I was on my way to flunking seventh grade.

In a 13-year-old's world, those are all the important people. And no one liked me.

I remember I had been seriously angry with God before this. For example, during my first days of playing football on the playground, I was struggling to keep up with my friends. I was doing my best, but then I came down with an asthma attack.

My friends not only had arms and legs, but they could breathe better than me, too. How fair was that?

Eventually, I learned how to deal with it through pacing myself and through medicine to relieve the asthma. But I feel my anger was justified and it was constructive. It helped me realize that life wasn't going to be fair.

By getting through that phase of anger, I was able to begin to understand God's purpose for me. I was going to have to work harder than most to overcome that unfairness.

This wheelchair thing was different. My spirit had finally met its match. I had been able to overcome all the other obstacles, but I had begun thinking of my motorized wheelchair as my legs, one of the first keys to my independence.

When I lost my chair, I had lost my legs. For the first time in my life, I was becoming handicapped, a foreign concept to me. I never felt handicapped before.

And, without friends or family, I couldn't think of a single reason for me to stay on this planet.

To make things worse, in science class, I had learned a ridiculously simple way to make poison. I could be dead so easily.

I mixed the stuff together and left it in my bedroom overnight. The second night, too, I slept with a glass of poison within reach. Then a third night.

I can't explain what made me pour that poison out. I know I didn't want my parents or my sister to deal with the pain of my death. I hadn't had a girlfriend. I felt at that time, this was one of the good things coming up in my life that I had not experienced yet.

I would like to say I read something or heard a voice that told me that my life should not be wasted.

But, hey, I'm mostly a visual guy. The message came in an image that I had developed out of this depression I was going through.

I saw myself as a rubber Super Ball speeding

downward. The closer I got to rock bottom, the sooner I would hit solid ground.

The bounce would be something to see. After I hit rock bottom there would be nowhere to go but up. I would soar faster and higher than anyone could ever dream.

I wanted to be around to see that.

CHAPTER THREE

"Strike three, but you're not out. When we put in 110 percent effort at the third try and we have not accomplished what we set out to do, most of us stop. We tell ourselves, I just gave my best three times, so I must not be able to do it. This is simply not true. Never stop at anything you want, especially on the third try. Once you have given up, that is when it is over."

— Brett Eastburn

KIDS IN MY ERA LEARNED how to play outdoors. We created our own fun. We made our own rules for games we played together. We spent a lot of time figuring out how to make and keep friends.

This was before the computers and electronic game systems hijacked children's minds. If I had been born in 1980 instead of 1970, maybe I would have spent my days indoors with Nintendo's Mario Brothers instead of outdoors with the kids next door.

The only electronic games I remember playing as a kid was Pong.

Blip. Blip. Blip. Blip. It certainly wasn't the sort of thrilling game that could keep our attention for hours. When you lived in an area full of kids, it didn't take much creativity to come up with a better game than that.

Don't get me wrong. I eventually played all those games. Gaming has its place, just not 24 hours a day.

By the time I was 11, we had moved from a farm outside North Liberty to a neighborhood in town, about a block from my school. That's when I started getting involved in sports.

People I meet have a hard time believing that I played all the sports they enjoyed as kids. That's because they're looking at the world through their eyes instead of mine.

There are at least two things they need to know about people like me.

Here's one: I don't believe in the adage "three strikes and you're out."

For some things, I might need a thousand tries to figure out how to succeed. I don't have hands and fingers to grip a baseball bat, so I hold the bat under my left armpit and use my midsection to swing at a ball.

Eventually, I'll figure out how to get the bat around at exactly the right time to hit the ball. But if I quit after just three tries, nothing good happens.

People talk all the time about giving extra effort. Give 150 percent of yourself. That's OK, but it's more important to be persistent. Try again and again and again and again, learning each time so you can try it differently the next.

Three swings won't do it.

The second thing people need to know is that I don't have to be able to do everything in order to help my team win.

I might pick one thing that I can do well. When my team needs me, I'm there and I'm ready with that one special skill.

Think about that in your own life. Are you trying to do too much by yourself? Wouldn't you be better off doing something that's within your power and letting the next guy swing for the fences?

No one, not even Barry Bonds, can hit a grand slam unless someone else fills the bases first.

Oh, and there's a third thing. If I want something,

I ask for it. It's never been society's obligation to ask me if I want to play baseball or to create a special team or sport for me. If I want to play a sport, any sport, I'll find a team and ask to join it.

That's what happened with Little League baseball. All my friends were going to play T-ball, and I figured I would too.

I learned how to swing a bat. I could hit the ball and hop to first base. When I got to the pitched-ball stage, I learned that I had an advantage over my teammates. I basically had the smallest, lowest strike zone any pitcher had ever seen.

In addition, the pitcher always had to worry about hitting the poor, little limbless guy, which made pitching to me even harder.

So, when our team needed a man on base, I was their guy. And if the pitcher was accurate enough to throw strikes, I could swing the bat just well enough to hit the ball between their infielders.

No one expected me to get a hit. So I had the surprise factor working for me.

I tried football for a while, too. If you think about the rules of football, you'll realize the unique advantage I had there.

Usually, a runner is considered down when his knee touches the ground. I don't have a knee. I would never be down.

I would hit the ground, bounce up and keep

going. So they changed the rule in games I played. I was down whenever my shoulder hit the ground.

I'm a fast hopper, but I don't have the ability to run long distances. My team figured out I was a sure thing for a yard every time I ran the ball. I was their short-yardage specialist.

One of the turning points for me was when I joined the school basketball team. As hard as I tried, I never figured out how to shoot a jump shot. When you're 2-foot-10½, that 10-foot basket is a long way away.

My fifth-grade teacher, Tim Davis, was coaching our elementary school team. I think I surprised him when I told him I wanted to join the basketball team. I know I was surprised when he told me I could.

If you grow up in Indiana, you know how to play basketball. I had been dribbling and passing long before I tried out for the team. If you can dribble and pass, you can be the point guard.

And that's what I was. I was quick enough to move the ball up court, and I knew how to get the ball to a teammate who could score.

Basically, I learned two key moves. If a defender came at me to steal the ball, I would use my right arm to whip a pass around him to a teammate. Once the defender figured out I could do that, he might try to over-react to my right. That's when I would fire a bounce pass right through his legs.

I didn't need to score. My teammates were doing that for us.

I didn't ask for any special treatment from the referees or my opponents. I remember one time an opponent just wrestled the ball away from me to get the winning shot, and the crowd booed him for it. His team wasn't happy about it either. You could tell it bothered him.

I just told him after the game not to worry about it. "You did what you're supposed to do," I told him. "That's why you're on the other team." Ricky Fosler and I have been good friends since that game.

In other sports, sometimes I felt my teammates and opponents all were giving me special treatment. They were carrying or coddling me. In basketball, finally, I felt like the games were legitimate. Both teams were trying their best to win.

Whether I had arms and legs or not, your job was to stop me.

But no sport made me feel like a real athlete until I started wrestling. I was in the fourth grade when I saw my first wrestling team. The high school team worked out in the gym after school. I would stick around and watch what they were doing.

It was almost an instant revelation that this would be my sport. It was perfect, in my eyes. You're on a team, but it's a one-on-one competition.

Wrestling is intense. If someone slacks off there, they end up with their shoulders on the mat. They lose. The wrestler who works the hardest wins.

Wrestling also is a sport that gave me a slight advantage over other kids. There's less of me to grab, so the techniques you use against another opponent will have to be adjusted when you wrestle against me.

Wrestling also rewards quickness, agility and upper body strength, all attributes that I had been working on ever since I hopped out of my first chair as a toddler.

So here I was, this little kid hanging around the wrestling room, watching the high school team. It wasn't long before I decided I wanted in on the action.

I would wait until one of the guys wasn't paying attention. Then I would pounce on him, like some wild animal. At the most basic level, I was learning what they would have to do to shake me loose.

It might have seemed like a joke to them at first. Eventually, though, they would realize that I wasn't going to let go without a battle. My grip might start to hurt. They might wonder if this little maniac with no arms or legs was actually going to pin them.

And they started wrestling, just to get away from me. That's how my career started.

By the time I started my freshman year at John Glenn High School, I had a personal goal. Any student who lettered in two sports would get a free letter jacket. I could get one letter by serving as manager on the football team. If I could earn my second letter in wrestling, I would get that free jacket.

The wrestling coach, Gene Bailey, told me later that he figured my interest in wrestling was just a passing fancy. He was going to let me practice, learn how difficult the sport would be and then expect me to move on to something else.

But by the middle of my freshman year, he realized I was in it for the long haul.

I weighed about 85 pounds at the time, which put me in the lowest weight class. I would be competing against kids who weighed a maximum of 103 pounds.

In most cases, those were the youngest, skinny kids with toothpicks for arms and legs. By the time they got out of high school with their adult bodies, they likely would grow to be 150 or so pounds.

By contrast, through all the work I had put my body through, I had developed grown-up muscles. I had the torso of someone weighing 130 pounds or more. I was just streamlined, without the longer arms and legs. So, in a sense, I was wrestling kids smaller than me.

In the early stages, many of those little guys were beating me. I might have the muscles, but I hadn't learned how to use them to win wrestling matches.

I stuck with it. In addition to wrestling at John Glenn, I competed in freestyle wrestling through the Amateur Athletic Union. In effect, I was wrestling almost year-round.

It's one thing to be wrestling against friends and neighbors you've grown up with. To them, I was just Brett. But when you compete in high school and AAU matches, you sometimes run across a different type of person.

We realized some wrestlers wouldn't want to compete against me. Kids can be a bit squeamish about touching a person like me. They think I'm contagious. If they touch me, their arms and legs might fall off.

Hey, I've met adults who have treated me the same way. It's fear borne out of ignorance. But the way to overcome fear is to confront it. Wrestle with it. Defeat it.

That's one of the reasons I had a special letter written for me that I carried to all my matches. Signed by the state wrestling association, it stated that I was qualified to compete. If a coach or opponent refused to wrestle against me, I would win by forfeit.

By the time I hit my junior year, I started to win more matches than I lost. I was beginning to use my experience to my advantage. Also, because I had been held back a year in elementary school, I was 18 years old, competing against skinny kids who usually were 14 or 15.

With the help of my coaches, I had come up with a special move, a modified version of the trap-and-roll.

It works something like this: An opponent would reach to put his arm around my little arm and their hand on the back of my neck. You've heard of it. It's called a Half Nelson. As soon as I felt his hand touch the back of my neck, I would clamp his elbow under my arm. Then I would jerk my shoulder down violently, flinging him over onto the mat.

Once I had mastered the move, the word got out quickly. You didn't want to wrestle "The Stub." If you did, you were going to get hurt.

I hit my peak during the AAU season of my junior year. I qualified for the national finals in Indianapolis, finishing fourth in the nation overall in the 98-pound class.

It was a big deal. The top couple wrestlers likely would be invited to compete on the U.S. Olympic team. I ended up a win or two away from accomplishing that.

When you get to that level, you realize how driven the top competitors are. No matter how many hours you've put in, there's someone across the mat from you who has put in as much, if not more.

My physical development and experience weren't enough at that level. I lost. When you hop away from a moment like that, you have questions. Did I really give my best effort? Could I have dug a little deeper and fought a little harder? Could I have held on for two minutes more?

The standing ovation in the Hoosier Dome caught me by surprise. Finally, I realized they were cheering for me, even though I had lost the match, placing me fourth in the nation.

I had wanted to win. I expected to. But in the end, I felt very satisfied. I was proud of what I had accomplished. Just getting into that final four in my weight class was a dream come true.

I didn't get a chance to go back the next year. I had reached age 20, and the lowest weight class for my age group was 110. I applied for a waiver to compete with the younger kids at 98 pounds again, but it wasn't allowed.

My dedication, training and bag of tricks worked well against the 98-pounders. But at 110, I would be facing the lean, mean killing machines.

I'm brave, but I'm not crazy. It was time to move on.

I'll have to admit that my success in wrestling—and the other sports I participated in—helped open doors for me. I now had it in my mind that someday I wanted to be a public speaker, to use my life as a positive example for others.

Until I began wrestling, I wasn't sure what that example would be.

I'm not a saint. I can't heal the sick or make the blind see. I wasn't an excellent student. Far from it, I've struggled in school, probably because of my dyslexia. But in any case, a career opportunity that had not been open to my grandparents and parents was available to me. I had to seize upon it.

I wasn't going to be a doctor, an engineer, or an astronaut either.

My example wasn't going to be about curing cancer or inventing the first flying car. My challenges are physical. And accomplishing what I did, in what is one of the most physically demanding of all sports, gives me some real credibility, mentally as well.

So I've got that going for me. I can talk the talk because I've walked the walk—in my own style, of course.

CHAPTER FOUR

"Most people make the mistake of trying to do an entire project at once, no matter what the job. Break it down into simpler tasks. Take things one step at a time, one piece at a time. You'll be surprised at how easy it becomes." — Brett Eastburn

IN LIFE, MANY CONSEQUENCES result from a single decision.

In the moment I bounced off my high chair and started exploring the world on my own, I basically decided I would choose an independent life.

So it never occurred to me that I could ever sit back and let someone else earn money for me. I was going to work, just like everyone else.

My first entrepreneurial experience, in second or third grade, got me into trouble with my mother.

She had been doing laundry when she found wads of money I had left in my pants pocket. I thought she would be proud of me when I told her how I was using my brain to make money. She wasn't.

At school, my classmates had been fascinated with my motorized wheelchair. Wherever I went, they would try to hop on the back to take a ride. They were like houseflies. As soon as I would shoo one off, another would land.

Finally, I decided to go into business. Anyone who brought an extra lunch dollar to school could buy a wheelchair ride during recess. I'm guessing I made about $20 before Mom discovered my stash.

She figured I was riding off with other kids' lunch money, so she put a stop to it.

I suppose my first legitimate job then was mowing our lawn. My grandfather gave me a riding lawn tractor and figured I would learn how to use it.

Eventually, my dad found out he could seat me up on the mower seat, put the tractor in gear and come back an hour or so later when the mowing was done. Dad decided to test me to see if I was going to be safe on a huge riding mower, and so he played a dirty little trick. He put me on the mower and fell down on purpose in front of it to make sure I knew how to stop it in time. It scared the crap out of me and made me incredibly mad. I see how he thought that it was the best way to see if I could stop the stupid thing in time so I wouldn't run into the house or a person. But it really pissed me off. I was able to stop in time by kicking the shifter into neutral. It was funny back then, not to me, but at least we can all laugh at it now.

Soon after that, Dad figured out that a farm tractor didn't drive any differently than a lawn tractor. So he would put me on our Case tractor, slip it into gear and walk away while I plowed our farm field.

Dangerous? Maybe. But I was no more likely to fall off than any other farmer. I loved driving that tractor. It made me feel useful. With me behind the wheel, Dad could spend a couple hours getting other chores done around the farm.

When we moved into town, I didn't have farm jobs anymore, but I was able to get a job one summer as a custodial engineer (janitor) at the school. It wasn't as glamorous as being a motivational speaker, comedian or actor, but it kept me plenty busy.

They gave me a dust mop, and because of my electric chair it took me half the time to clean the floor. Then they had me clean out the bottom of every student locker in the building. When I was done with that, they had me scrape all the chewing gum from under the desks and tables. I would use Freon to freeze the gum, making it easier to scrape. We didn't know then that Freon damages the ozone layer. Can't use that stuff any more in this day and age.

That job had quite an effect on me. I began to realize that the simplest things kids do would create work for someone else. Afterwards, whenever I would see a classmate shoot a spitwad or drop a scrap of paper in school, I would ask them to clean it up.

For the next couple years, I considered my sports career as my summer job. But I knew I wouldn't make much money as a wrestler. I had a sense that I wanted to spend my life sharing my story with other people. I just didn't know how to go about doing that.

At this point in my life, I wasn't sure what I would end up doing for a living. A lot of people thought I would become a professional artist.

I had begun drawing, like every kid does, before I started school. You've probably seen quadriplegics draw by using a pencil holder clenched between their teeth. That's not the way I do it. I squeeze the pencil between my little arm and my chin. Sometimes I get cross-eyed because my face is so close to my drawing paper, but that's how I do it.

And because I was interested in it, I became quite good at it. By the time I was in high school, my work was winning local contests and was being sent to national competitions.

I mainly drew portraits. The real secret to my success was that I wasn't afraid to draw. A lot of beginners worry that they will mess up. You miss on one little detail and you end up scrapping the whole project—I learned this thanks to my advanced art class teacher. Quit on enough projects and eventually you'll stop drawing altogether.

Drawing, to me, is like everything else. You take a difficult job and break it into smaller pieces. Most of us can't start out by drawing a face accurately. But almost anyone can draw a circle. You take that circle and make little changes in it until you have the face you're looking for.

At that stage in my life, I spent a lot of time making drawings of myself. I guess it was my way then to tell people who I was. I wasn't a speaker or a word guy yet. I wanted people to know my story, and my outlet was art.

One of my award-winning drawings was of two wrestlers, one American and the other Russian. What interested the contest judges the most was that I drew an artificial leg on the Russian. Maybe the judges thought I was making a political comment by doing

47

that. But what really happened is, I was looking through a magazine for reference photos. And there I saw this snazzy new prosthetic leg, made out of titanium. I just added it to the drawing.

I've made a little money off my art. For a while, I would take old circular saw blades and paint scenes on them. It would take me 15 to 20 minutes to finish one, and I would sell them for $10 apiece at the local Potato Creek Festival.

I think my intense interest in art became more of a hobby than a moneymaker when I found a new challenge—playing pool. When I play pool, I want to play against all types of people, not just those who have disabilities. I use a self-modified cue stick that helps me with my grip, but other than that I play by the same rules as everybody else. I don't want any special breaks.

Pool is my passion now, in addition to my career. I'm guessing I'll stay with it longer than some of the other things. That's because it's such a difficult game to master. I play well enough to beat the majority of the people I play. But there are always people out there who know something I don't know.

My wife Chrisa is one of the top-ranked women pool players in our region. It's a game that doesn't favor people who are taller, stronger or faster, so women and men can play on a fairly even level. When she and I play, I usually win. I think it's because I want to win. For her, the game is fun. For me, it's more like a fun war.

I suppose I put my art supplies away because I didn't have the passion anymore. I realized I had a bigger message to convey that my drawings wouldn't deliver. I needed words to tell the story, so I threw my whole self into finding those words and getting them to sound just right.

When I have more time, I'll take up drawing and painting again. I'll make room for a studio. It's a talent you never really lose.

CHAPTER FIVE

"No matter how many times I've given a speech, I'm afraid I'll forget my spot. No matter how many laughs my jokes have gotten, I'm afraid my comedy act is going to bomb. That's when I think of my 200-year timeline theory. Two hundred years from now, are the small things that I worried about going to stand out? I know in the long run, the silly things that I worry about won't matter. So I can stop worrying and finish the job with no regrets."

— Brett Eastburn

EVERYTHING CHANGED FOR ME at an all-school assembly during my junior year at John Glenn High School.

Bill Essex, a former undercover police investigator, was going to speak to us. I planned on taking a two-hour nap. Why would I want to listen to this guy?

What followed were two of the most interesting hours of my life.

Bill was very personable. He was fun. His stories about his undercover experiences were fascinating. But it was more than that.

He respected us. He wasn't talking down to us like he was the expert and we were a bunch of ignorant kids. He won us over, and those two hours just flew by. This was the moment that made me realize that this was going to be the way I would tell people about my message.

As soon as his talk was over, I went up to the stage to talk with Bill. I told him I wanted to do what he was doing. He was polite, and he asked me to write him a letter explaining why I wanted to be a public speaker.

Normally, I wouldn't have written anyone a letter. It wasn't that I didn't like to write. I'm like everyone else. I'm lazy at some things. But I couldn't wait to get that letter started. I wanted to tell Bill what my message was and ask him how to get it out.

Before I knew it, Bill had a business partner. Me. For the next seven years, I was an employee of Essex Educational Services.

I learned the business the same way others learn how to be plumbers or welders. I served an apprenticeship, following Bill to speaking engagements throughout the Midwest.

Mainly, I listened. Time after time, he would present the same program in virtually the same words. And for me, despite dozens of times watching from backstage, the program never got old. That's how good he was.

The time I spent on the road with him also gave me a chance to work out the basics of my own "No Arms, No Legs, No Handicaps!" presentation. My goal was to take my ideas and make them sound as interesting as Bill's.

If you've ever attended my program, you'll probably remember that I tell a couple of funny stories and perform some demonstrations. Maybe that's all you will get out of it, an hour of unique entertainment.

But more than likely, you'll also walk away from the program feeling a little better about yourself. You should have a sense that maybe the obstacles in front of you aren't as big as they once seemed.

That's because, with Bill's help, I've put several key principles into my speech. And though I continually tweak the program, those are the same principles that I started out with in 1990. Each piece of the speech ties into the principles that I live by and speak about.

After months of watching Bill from backstage, he suddenly told me it was time to debut my program.

All these years later, the details of that first speech are hazy. I remember the setting was a picnic shelter in a park, and I was going to speak to a youth group of some sort. I had a bit of an anxiety attack there as I realized I had an entire hour to fill.

I wrote my main points on a recipe card. I brought a basketball and a football to use as part of the demonstrations. And feeling the pure fear of not knowing what I would say, I just began speaking.

I'm sure I've given better programs over the years, and I'm sure I've given worse. But the most important thing about that presentation was that I got through it. Bill wasn't there. He knew it was my first big program, and he knew I needed to do it on my own.

It also was real money for me. I would get a portion, and the rest would go to the company. Eventually, my share grew as my reputation spread and people began asking specifically for me.

I'm grateful that Bill gave me the start. He showed me the ins and outs of public speaking and, three years before I left the company in 1998, I was named Essex Educational Services' vice president at 23 years old. Not bad for a guy who didn't get straight A's in high school.

I left the company when Bill got ready to retire.

He wanted me to take over the business, but it wasn't really what I needed to do. It didn't fit my view of how a company should work. He had set the thing up as a non-profit organization. In addition to bringing in speaking fees, he had fundraisers and a grant writer. I didn't want to ask for donations. I felt that I needed to go out on my own.

When I went into business for myself, it was going to be a for-profit S-Corp thing. I was going to make it on my speaking talent alone.

All these years later, it's easy to get a little cynical about the business side of public speaking. At the very base, a speaker is just a time filler. An event organizer has an hour set aside for a speech, and it's our job to make it happen.

The requirements are few. Show up a half-hour early so the organizer doesn't get a stiff neck looking out the window for you. Be in a good mood. Say something interesting. Leave when your time is up.

Unfortunately, a lot of speakers meet the minimum requirement but don't go beyond it. Their feeling is that, as long as no one complains after the speech, you have a good chance of getting invited back. So the whole goal of the speech is to avoid making anyone uncomfortable.

I have to remind myself that I didn't go into this line of work to make money. My goal was to make a difference. That's a lot to ask from a one-hour presentation, but I think it can be done.

I call it the Johnny Appleseed approach. You drop the message into the ground and you move on. It's not your place to stick around and make sure there's a harvest. We just bring the seed.

I doubt that any of this had occurred to me before the day that Bill Essex showed up in my high school auditorium. I just thought I had an interesting story to tell, and somehow, someday I would tell it.

As it turned out, my connection with Bill turned my final months at John Glenn into a whirlwind. I kept up with my schoolwork while I also was traveling and speaking on weekends.

So, when it came time to graduate, I was more than ready to go.

I had overcome so much to be successful in so many ways.

My teachers never realized how hard I had tried. But with dyslexia, I just couldn't process written words like everyone else. It took me six or seven times to read a paragraph before I would digest the information you might get in a single reading. For me, it was an added effort for the info to stick.

It was like giving me a newspaper printed in Japanese, telling me to read it and expecting me to discuss it in detail tomorrow. I tried. I had success; but I was tired of school.

I was ready to move on to the next challenge. I would be learning different things in different ways. I had friends getting ready for college, but I felt in some ways I was already ahead of them. I wasn't just chasing a dream. As a professional public speaker, I was living it already.

One interesting thing happened to me before graduation.

I started getting phone calls from a military recruiter. He had compiled some information about me, and what he had read made him think I was just what America needed.

On the phone, I would just tell him, "I don't think you want me," but I wouldn't tell him why.

About the fourth time he called, he became a little more insistent. He said he knew I had been a decent student, had played some basketball and wrestled. He said the military could help me find some direction in life.

"You'll do great," he said. "And we can pay for your college, too."

It had gone on long enough. It was time to tell him. I said, "I don't have arms and legs, dude."

"Oh. Sorry." Click.

CHAPTER SIX

"Almost no one becomes a success overnight. In fact, I may never get to the place I've imagined for myself. But I'm enjoying the process of trying to get there. If today is the best I'll ever be, I'm thankful for the cool stuff I have, the interesting places I've been and the amazing people I've met. I am just playing the hand I was dealt."

— Brett Eastburn

I HAD LEARNED A COUPLE OF IMPORTANT THINGS by the time I graduated from high school.

One, the Army and the Marines weren't going to take me.

And two, I had to get out of town.

It's not that my childhood was so bad. Even as an obstinate 19-year-old, I realized I had been luckier than a lot of guys I knew. My parents went above and beyond to make sure I had the opportunity to chase my dreams.

And I certainly couldn't complain about the way my hometown treated me. Wherever I went, people accepted me the way I was.

But my dreams weren't going to stop at the North Liberty town limits. Somehow, I had this vision of going places, meeting people and changing their lives.

There was another reason to leave, too, and it wasn't nearly as noble. I didn't like having a curfew. My parents didn't want me to be out all night. My friends all seemed to be able to come and go whenever they liked. I was old enough, I thought, that I shouldn't have grown-ups telling me to be in bed by midnight.

If I wanted to escape my childhood, all I needed was a job, a car and a place to stay.

I had the job, with Essex. I took out a $5,000 loan and my parents took out a second mortgage so I could buy myself a van.

If it sounds a bit dangerous for a guy with no arms or legs to be driving an E150 full-sized van, it's not a problem at all. But it is expensive. We needed to add a wheelchair ramp and had to modify the controls so I could activate the brakes and the gas pedal with my stubs. After some pushing, Indiana's Vocational Rehabilitation Services paid a portion of the costs. They make sure that folks like me can get and maintain jobs to support themselves. My modified van would be the step needed for employment.

So, I had my wheels and I had my career mapped out with Bill Essex, who was training me to be a public speaker. The best spot for me to do that would be Indianapolis.

I grabbed a couple of my school buddies and convinced them to move to Indianapolis with me. Our first place wasn't much to brag about. Basically, we were going to live in a trailer park.

My parents weren't too thrilled with my plan. Looking back on it, I can't blame them. I was joining up with Essex, but I was going to be paid more like a part-time intern. Self-confidence is one thing, and I had plenty, but a steady paycheck might be more important in the long term.

I'm certain I wasn't the first person to discover life in the real world is a little tougher than I expected. I didn't get rich or famous. Instead, I got frustrated and a bit angry.

I went in with my eyes open and aware of the risk

involved in going to work for a non-profit business. I suppose most non-profits struggle to get the bills paid. As a result, employees have to wait their turn for their money.

One of my goals at first was to figure out how the business ran. Bill eventually would retire, and I would take over. Maybe then I would start making enough money to live the way I expected to.

But days turned into weeks, and weeks turned into years.

I want to be careful about not complaining too much about that first step in my career. I have so much to be grateful for. Without that first meeting with Bill, I don't know if I ever would have been able to develop my interest in public speaking. And all the while I was working in Indianapolis, I was training for the day when I could start my own business.

I knew I wasn't going to work in his company forever, just as I wasn't going to live in Mom and Dad's house forever. I would grow up and move on. Some lessons you learn only by struggling with them. That's what I think, anyway.

One of the great moments in my life came while I was still with Bill.

Every year, he would go to the International PRIDE conference. It's a huge deal. A large part of the audience includes educators from around the world, and one year I ended up on the main stage.

It was in Texas, and I found myself in front of 10,000 people. I had only a few minutes to present my program, which typically runs a full hour. But on that stage, I began to realize how it's possible to reach far beyond the several hundred or so students I was used to seeing in school gyms.

I also learned that it's just as easy, maybe even easier, to address 10,000 people than it is to address 10. Later, I found that's especially true in comedy clubs. Three sourpusses in the front row of a small club or school auditorium can totally kill a performance. But the larger the crowd, the easier it is to find a few people to smile or laugh.

Sometimes you can hear the small laughs ripple through an audience and feel the whole mood of the place change.

Laugh at me once and I'll get you the next time, too. And your neighbor. And the guy next to him. Laughter is contagious. It really is true: The more, the merrier.

My four minutes on the PRIDE stage in Houston were a large boost in my speaking career. But that wasn't the great moment I mentioned earlier. Like so many other things in life, it was just the spark that lit a bigger fuse.

In the audience was a person connected with the Department of Defense schools in Japan. He liked what he saw in me, and he invited me to come to Japan for two weeks.

For a guy from North Liberty, this was a big deal. Basically, I was supposed to speak at the Department of Defense schools, which are for the sons and daughters of the people serving on the military bases.

I didn't have to learn Japanese. I would be giving the same program I might give to the kids in Indiana, except that I would be doing it halfway around the world.

In Japan, I got a chance to try new things. Iced coffee, for example, was on the menus at McDonald's there long before our fast-food restaurants here started offering it. Cold noodles. Octopus. Sushi. Sometimes you need to get outside your comfort zone.

While I was there, I had a chance to meet with a support group for Japanese people with disabilities. For that one, I needed an interpreter. We talked about the differences between how Americans and Japanese traditionally look at disabilities.

One of the things I learned was that, in the traditional Japanese culture, people often believe that birth defects occur because of a parent's sins.

I left them with my usual message that there is no shame involved with being disabled and that people with disabilities need to be persistent and inventive to get what they want. I've had a lot of success talking with disability awareness groups just like that.

At the end of the presentation, dinner was served. It was a chicken and rice dish. With chopsticks. No fork.

I could feel that every eye in the room was on me.

Would I give up and ask for a fork? I puzzled with it for a second and caught a glimpse of my hosts grinning at me. I grabbed a stick between both my arms, stabbed a piece of chicken and said, "Aha," before I ate it.

That brought my biggest applause of the night. I think they were polite enough not to notice that I didn't eat any of my rice. You just can't stab a grain of rice with a chopstick.

But my absolute biggest moment in Japan came at another event. In Japan at that time, most children with disabilities were sent to segregated schools, just for disabled kids. At those schools, there were facilities and teachers that had specific training for those with disabilities.

The schools probably did a nice job, but to me, it didn't seem right. You should have a choice, like I did. If you want to take your chances in a public school, that should be up to you.

I didn't go there expecting to say that to these students and their parents. But I did. I also said the system wasn't going to change unless someone in that room spoke up against it, because the majority in your society thinks that you are where you belong.

If you want to go to a public school, you're going to have to fight for the right.

Well, I said it, and then I left the country.

Sometime later, I got a package from Japan that included a few of their newspapers. Everything was written in Japanese, which I obviously couldn't read. But someone had included an English translation, which said three families had successfully sued the public school system so their special-needs students could be mainstreamed.

As I read it, I cried.

I had always wanted to help bring change to the world, and not just to my little corner of it. Like Johnny Appleseed.

I was glad that someone sent me those papers. It was one of those bright spots that kept my spirit fed during the Essex period, when I was struggling with money and was unhappy with the direction of the company. I was feeling less and less like an inspirational speaker.

My parents had heard plenty about my frustrations in Indianapolis. They knew I was stubborn about it. I was dedicated to the dream and it wasn't going to be easy for me to admit that I wasn't going to succeed.

Finally, after five years, I asked if I could come home. I needed their help to do it.

I had thought of quitting the business many times. But Bill, through his years of persuasive speaking, knew how to draw me back.

This time, my family helped me load up everything I owned before I told Bill I was leaving. My bags were packed. I was ready to go. And I left.

CHAPTER SEVEN

"People who believe in handicaps are constantly creating obstacles for themselves. They are allowing themselves to stop, to quit, to settle for less than they deserve. Everyone's life has difficult spots. People place handicaps on others or themselves. If we consciously remove the obstacles, those are times you have a chance to grow and to learn new ways to do things."

— Brett Eastburn

IN SOME WAYS, I WAS AT ONE of the low points in my life, a real tail-between-my-legs kind of thing.

I had left North Liberty filled with confidence, vowing that I was going to make my life in the big city and travel the world. And here I was, moving back into my parents' house, just down the block from my old elementary school.

It was hard not to feel small.

I still would get an occasional call asking me to give a speech, and I had my monthly Social Security payments coming in, but I knew I couldn't live the rest of my life just cashing those checks for groceries and gas. I started looking around for other things I could do. And I vowed that my life would be interesting and have meaning.

One of the jobs I took to make ends meet was with a company that cleared trees from the banks of creeks and the Yellow River. The company was owned by a man from North Liberty who knew about my abilities to overcome any obstacles, so he realized he wasn't taking a major risk hiring someone without arms and legs.

For a guy like me who loves big machinery, this was a really cool job. Basically, I controlled the boom truck. Other workers would cut the trees with chain saws and I would swing the big arm and cable over to them. After they attached the cable around the tree, I would use the boom to lift it away from the river bank.

It was a hugely dangerous and responsible job. There were four or five guys running around on the ground. If I made a mistake with the boom at any given time, the tree or cable might swing around and kill one of those guys. But as dangerous as it was, it wasn't a job that required arms and legs. It was all about eyes and brains.

It was a matter of paying close attention to everything that was going on.

Another job I had was as a greeter at a major discount store. I didn't exactly love that job. I would sit there, making $5.50 an hour, thinking about how long it was going to take me to get the same amount I could have earned with a single speech. But I had bills to pay, and those speech deals weren't always there.

Eventually, I became a store detective. I was the guy who was on the lookout for thieves and shoplifters. The main thing about that job was that it made me regret being so stubborn about not taking typing class in high school.

I had talked my way out of typing class, using the excuse that I didn't have fingers to place on the ASDF and JKL; home keys.

No fingers. It was an excuse I rarely used. If I had wanted to learn to type, I would have figured out a way, just as I learned to throw a football with no hands. The truth was, I simply didn't want to do it.

Keep in mind, this was the day of the typewriter and the word processor. No one, including me, was thinking that we would all be sitting in front of computer keyboards at home and at work or that even our telephones might require that we know how to type.

In the career I have now, I don't just sit and speak. I build my web site. I create brochures. Keyboarding is one of the most important things I do.

At the store, I had to learn the hunt-and-peck method for typing, which made my job so much harder. I might watch someone come into the store, grab the first item off the first shelf and try to run with it. Our staff and I would catch him, and it would all be over in a couple minutes. But it would take me two hours or more just to type a report on the incident. It was so slow.

Now there are voice-recognition programs that can do the typing for you. I've used those some. But I really started learning to type when I began using instant messaging online. It was fun. It made me want to learn.

I like challenges, so I liked running the boom truck, and I liked being a store detective. But those weren't Johnny Appleseed jobs. I wasn't done with the dream.

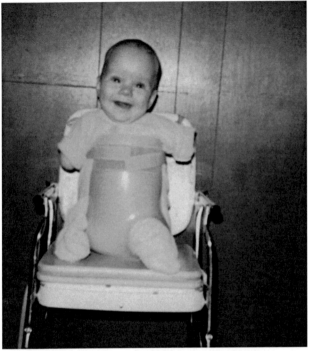

As an infant I had to wear a brace to allow me to sit up

Mom, he's looking at me

Halloween with my Dad

When I was a toddler, I wore prosthetics

Fishing with Dad

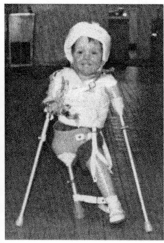

Passing the ball

Dribbling up the court

North Liberty Elementary Basketball Team

Halftime pep talk

Woodshop Class

Welding Class

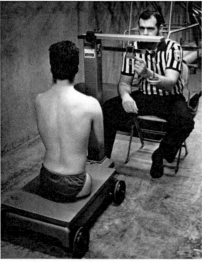

Weighing in

Waiting for the next match

Talking to am opponent

Coach Bailey

Inflicting pain

Me and Chad King at a wrestling match

I wish I still looked like this

Sparring

Rolling in on my skareboard.

One step at a time.

The love of my life...Chrisa

Murray.

Piloting a sub; Aruba Tour; Panama Tour

Watercolor painting of wrestlers awarded honorable mention

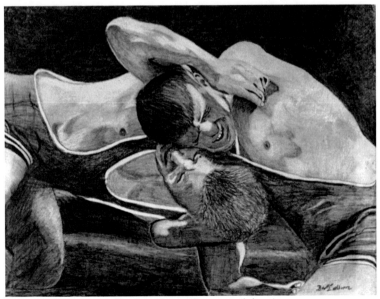

Chad and I wrestling, pencil drawing

Portrait of Terri.

Self-portrait.

Scratchboard.

Scratchboard 1998

My sister Krista

CHAPTER EIGHT

"I am better than no one, and no one is better than I. It's easy to feel intimidated when someone else uses their social or career status to put you down. For someone like me, people of all sorts feel superior, that they have something I can't get or that I can't do. You hear them say, "I feel so sorry for you." Forget that. No one is better than I am, and I am no better than they."

— Brett Eastburn

WE ARE ALL UNIQUE. Some of us seem "more unique" than others because of how we look. And there are times when you think no one on earth has had to put up with what I'm going through.

But then you run across a story that humbles you. In my case, there's the one about Arthur MacMorrough Kavanagh.

He was born without arms and legs in Ireland in 1831. He came from a wealthy family, so he didn't want to miss out on the good things in life.

He had a special saddle built so he could become an expert horseman. He also learned to fish, shoot, draw and write with his arm stumps.

There's quite a story about him that I read on a web site called The Long Riders' Guild. It's about a trip he and his older brother Tom took by horseback all the way across Europe to India via Moscow and Persia.

When they got there, Tom decided to take a boat back to Ireland, leaving Arthur on his own. During that voyage, Tom got sick and died. Arthur was stranded, alone and without money in India.

Arthur got a job as a government dispatch rider, the British Empire's version of the Pony Express. Eventually, he ended up back in Ireland, where he took over his father's estate, married, raised four children and served in the Parliament.

So if I ever start thinking about how amazing I am, being able to throw a football without any hands, I have to remember there was a guy born with stubs before me named Arthur MacMurrough Kavanagh.

He left big shoes to fill.

And there are times, too, when I find out about someone in my own era that is doing amazing things with even less than what I have.

As far as birth deformities go, I always thought I was close to the end of the scale, maybe even at the absolute extreme. Most people I've run across have at least one elbow or a knee. If you have one of those joints, it makes a huge difference in your ability to walk or use your arm. As far as I knew, inch for inch, I had the least in the way of extremities.

That was until I heard about Richard Devylder. You can find a video of him on the Internet. He was born with even less of his limbs than I have. Basically, he was born with a head and a torso. He has no stubs at all.

Like me, he seems to be doing very well. He's had a six-figure job in the California state government as an adviser on disability issues. His home in Sacramento has a backyard swimming pool, which he uses every day as his main source of exercise. He has a lift to get himself in and out of the water.

The joystick on his wheelchair is mounted so he can change directions simply by moving his shoulder.

It's a bit spooky for me, watching him on video. It's like seeing some long-lost relative you didn't know you had. And it makes me wonder whether he's seen videos of me doing my comedy act, and whether he feels the same way.

We'll have to get in touch.

The stories about Arthur and Richard are reminders that you can accomplish a lot if you take advantage of the resources that are available.

I'm sure there are others, too.

We all are unique, but it gives me strength to know there are people out there like me. In this electronic age, they feel like neighbors.

CHAPTER NINE

"I like being different. It sets me apart and opens me up for more positive attention. But some people are uncomfortable when they confront something new. One of the keys is to break the ice for people who may not be comfortable with you. Give them a reason to find out who you really are."

— Brett Eastburn

IF YOU'VE ATTENDED ONE OF MY SPEECHES in the last decade, you probably have met Murray. He's a collie/retriever mix, and he's named after the dog in the old "Mad About You" TV series.

Like most things in my life, Murray started out serving one purpose but has ended up doing something entirely different.

I had grown up with dogs. My parents had a series of little poodle-type dogs. When I was old enough to live on my own, I didn't especially want a pet. I had friends. I didn't need a dog to keep me company.

But then I started hearing about service dogs. A friend of mine told me that Fred Church, who lives in a town nearby, had been a trainer with the Midwest Assistance Dogs. Fred was retiring from that, but he told the friend that he would be willing to take on one more dog, if I really wanted one.

Sure, I could use a service dog, but over the years I had learned to do so many things for myself that I didn't want to rely on someone or something to do things for me. I couldn't imagine asking Fred to teach a dog to do the same things I've taught myself.

The breakthrough for me was when I realized a service dog isn't there to save your life. He's there to make your life a little easier, a little better.

Service dogs, like people, all are different. Murray, for example, was spending time at a Humane Society shelter when the employees thought he would make the perfect service dog. You might call him a mutt. Fred likes working with mixed breeds. They're often smarter and healthier than pure breeds because they don't have the genetic peculiarities that can accompany in-breeding.

Our first idea for Murray was that maybe he could pull me when I'm using a manual chair. It would be a lot like a Husky pulling a dogsled.

So, Fred and Murray worked on that for a while. After about five months, Murray had the concept, but we decided it wasn't going to be very useful. It was going to be too much work, for him and for me.

Every time I was going to let Murray pull me someplace, I was going to have to get him into a harness and get the whole thing hitched up to my chair. Usually, by the time I got all that accomplished, the mood would have passed to go somewhere. I would be better off staying home or using my power chair.

So we turned our training in another direction. Fred taught Murray some domestic stuff, like how to open a refrigerator and bring me a soft drink. It's worked out great.

There are other things Murray can do that I appreciate. On most days, if I drop my keys or my cell phone, I just lower myself out of my chair, grab whatever I've dropped, and bounce back up.

But when it's rained or during snowy weather,

I would end up with wet pants. With a simple voice command, I can get Murray to fetch what I've dropped, and I can stay out of the mud or snow. He's more than happy to help me out with that.

That's the routine I typically do when Murray comes with me to one of my programs. I bring him out early, introduce him, drop my keys, let him retrieve them for me, and send him offstage.

It's been a big crowd pleaser. He also would help demonstrate what to do when meeting a service dog and how to request permission to pet the animal or, for that matter, anyone's pet.

Over the years, I've realized that I really don't need Murray so much for household chores. I need him more for an educational tool. I want to help people understand what service dogs are and how they can help.

Let me tell you a couple things that service dogs are not.

They are not guard dogs. I suppose Murray would do his best to protect me if someone meant to do me harm. That's what friends are for. But if I really wanted a guard dog, I would go out and find a bigger, meaner dog and give the job to him.

They are not babe magnets. Sometimes a handsome pet can serve as a social icebreaker. It gives someone who is interested in you an excuse to stop and say hello. Murray's a good-looking guy, but he's not a pet. When he's with me, he's working. He's either doing a task or waiting for a command. He doesn't have time to eyeball women for me. And when I met my wife, Chrisa, by the way, Murray was nowhere around.

When you meet a service dog, you need to forget everything you've learned about dogs from "Lassie," "Rin Tin Tin," "Frasier" or Murray's favorite, "Mad About You."

When a working dog has on a work vest or harness, they drop into work mode. Never, ever approach the dog without the human companion's permission. The dog is not prepared to meet someone new. He's thinking of you as a barrier to completing his mission. If you ask for permission, it gives the dog and the owner time so they're no longer in a work state of mind.

There's another aspect about Murray that I hope comes across to the people he and I meet. That is, he has rights and privileges. If I'm allowed into your restaurant or business, so is he.

A lot of people don't get it, and I can't really blame them for being uncomfortable at first. Service dogs are rare enough that seeing one can throw you off-kilter. If you're in a restaurant or a store where pets are not allowed, you immediately think that anyone with a dog is violating the law.

Believe me in this: The person violating the law

is the one who tries to keep me and Murray out on the street. The Americans with Disabilities Act clearly states it. If you let other members of the public walk in, you have to let me roll in. And since Murray is there to assist me, he gets in too.

I try to be understanding about this. Like I've said, anyone who meets me, with or without Murray, for the first time usually has some information to process. If someone tells me Murray can't go inside their building, I try to be polite. But I have documents with me that show otherwise. Let us in, or face the consequences.

It's hard to qualify for a service dog. If you really need a dog, you can get one, but you have to go through an application process. In theory, I suppose it's possible for someone to pretend to be blind just so Rover can get into a four-star restaurant. But I doubt it ever really happens. If you see a service dog at work, you'll know the difference.

Having said that, I recognize that I call on Murray for help less and less often. In our time together, Murray probably has listened to my speech at least 2,000 times. I like to think of him as being semi-retired now.

As I write this, he is 13 years old, and finally we are able to think of him more as a family member than as an adaptive device or service dog. If he never hears another speech, that's fine with me. He deserves his rest.

I know it will be a sad day when Murray leaves us. In many ways, when he's not working, he's become our child. But even in his retirement years, when he sleeps, he keeps his head under my wheelchair. He wants to make sure that he's the first to know when I get ready to move.

CHAPTER TEN

"You're never stuck, you're just temporarily delayed." — Brett Eastburn

SPEAKING OF WHEELCHAIRS, LET'S ADDRESS THAT.

In an earlier chapter, I wrote about how traumatic it was in seventh grade when my motorized chair broke down. I became depressed. I felt helpless. I didn't want to go on living.

I look at things differently now, but I have to admit a strong sense of despair comes back whenever my chairs are on the fritz. Only with my chairs am I really free. Many of you feel the same about your car. If it breaks down, you have lost the freedom to go where you want when you want. It's the same thing with my chairs.

With my chairs, I can zip down the sidewalk to my van, drive to an airport and go anywhere in the world, pretty much by myself. Without my chairs, I need someone to help me at nearly every step of the way. You're never really free when you have to ask people for assistance all the time.

You'll note that I use the plural form "chairs." I've been a Boy Scout, so I know what it means to be prepared. I have a main chair and a spare. When one breaks down, it costs time and money to get it fixed. It's rare, but sometimes my chair and my spare both are broken. It happens to my vans, too. Whenever one loses a part, it seems like the other one goes on a sympathy strike.

I got my first motorized chair when I was in kindergarten. It wasn't much to look at, but it seemed like a big deal to me. Basically, it was a manual wheelchair with a battery-powered motor and a control device.

It had two speeds—go and stop. I could turn it left

or right. As primitive as it was, I felt like real hot stuff when I touched the controls. I was riding in style.

Nowadays, I compare those old chairs to the Yugo. If you've never been in a car before, you can like the Yugo. It gets you from one place to another more quickly than if you walked or crawled. But if you've ever had a better vehicle, you won't be caught dead in a Yugo.

Some folks might have a motorized chair that lasts up to five years, but most of my chairs last much longer than that—partly because there's nothing typical about me.

Wheelchair users come in all shapes and sizes, as well as all ranges of interests and mobility.

My chairs, like me, are constantly on the go but I take good care of them. If I give 200 speeches a year, that adds up to a lot of miles for the motors, bearings and tires. My chairs have been to most of the 50 states and to several foreign countries. They've taken a lot of beatings just getting in and out of airplanes and rented vans. Owning a chair is just like owning a car. There is a level of care that the chairs need that most people do not know how to do—or their insurance company won't foot the bill for the repair.

I get my chairs through insurance, when we have it, and through Vocational Rehabilitation.

Voc-Rehab is a nice tool for those who need extra

help in achieving goals of a better job or college. If you're born with a disability or acquire one later, there are a lot of ways for you to give up. Society doesn't expect a lot out of us. We have our good, obvious reasons why we can stay home and disappear into a day-long routine of TV shows.

When this program works right and is incorporated with people being clear with what they want, knowing their rights and working with a reasonable counselor, Voc-Rehab helps to strip away those excuses. It removes the words "I can't" from the equation. If I feel tired or lazy or afraid and I don't want to try something new, those are personal hurdles. I have to decide what kind of person I am. Do I sit or do I move?

You often hear of government programs that are big on red tape. They have everything you need or want, but they're going to make you jump through a lot of hoops to get it. They set standards hardly anyone can meet. They want to discourage you, slow you down or tackle you before you reach the goal line. Nursing homes are where young and old disabled people live because of the government's outdated policy of not paying for in-home care. Disability rights activists want nursing homes to cease to exist. Further, in different parts of the country, people who live in these nursing homes have sued the state because their nursing home will not pay for/buy a power wheelchair. I've met people who have been stuck lying in bed for years because the nursing home won't get the wheelchair. This practice is not humane and we need to make sure all people who need wheelchairs get them.

That certainly has not been my experience with Voc-Rehab. Maybe it's because I'm so clear on what I want to do. Whatever the reason, most of the time, I get a lot of help and I appreciate it.

I also have been impressed with the folks who make, sell and service wheelchairs. If I can tell them what I want, and I'm reasonable about it, they'll make sure I get it.

Sometimes, when I'm trying to get into a new chair, lowering a foot pedal by two inches or adding some kind of nylon strap will make all the difference. In most cases, if you can tell them what you need, the wheelchair folks can make it work.

That's the real lesson here: Take charge of things that matter to you.

A motorized wheelchair is like a body. It can make you tall, fast, sturdy, nimble—whatever you choose to be. It's the equivalent of deciding whether you want to be LeBron James or Shaquille O'Neal.

Me, I prefer speed and agility. The chairs they build now can go 12 miles per hour or more. They can turn on a dime. But I also can elevate the seat so I don't have to talk to someone eyeball to bellybutton. You are taken more seriously in the business world if you can look someone right in the eye. I also can slant the whole thing so I can take a nap during a two-hour wait at the airport. I can have headlights and turn signals.

All these options are there because people weren't content to sit in a simple chair with a battery-powered motor attached. They had ideas and spoke up.

A wide number of other factors out there are working in our favor. Part of this boom in technology goes back to the Sixties and the space race. A lot of the gadgets invented to get people safely on and off the moon led to the light but sturdy materials that go into my chair.

There's battlefield stuff here, too. A lot of young men have lost arms and legs during the wars in Vietnam and the Persian Gulf. When they came home, they weren't going to be satisfied with a Civil War-era peg leg. They wanted their old lives back, as best they could get them. They made their voices heard.

And there's this other thing. Today's inventors and engineers grew up with video games. No age group is content playing with their older brothers' and sisters' toys. If you look at the controls of modern wheelchairs, they're like video game joysticks. Driving one of these is like playing a game. In fact, I have to keep a close eye on that when I'm visiting elementary schools these days. If I glance away for a minute, some kid is likely to grab the stick and send me into a spin or shoot me across the room.

The kind of chairs I have typically cost upwards of $10,000. There are options that might be cool to have—for another $4,000.

It's easy to complain when things don't go perfectly, but sometimes you have to leave a situation to get a new perspective. That's the way it's been for me and the wheelchairs I use. There are places I've been in America where people really understand the need for wheelchair access. They take good care of their sidewalks and provide access ramps.

It's not just for people like me. These days, you see a lot more older people using scooters. For them, a scooter is a way to stay independent and active once their legs become too wobbly to walk. When the Americans with Disabilities Act (ADA) was passed and cities were required to put ramps on their sidewalks, many taxpayers complained. They wondered how many millions of dollars were going to be spent just so one or two people with wheelchairs could benefit.

They didn't realize how the ramps would help open up their businesses and restaurants to the older generation. It's a case where everybody can benefit. Anyone can walk up a ramp. A chair or scooter can't jump a curb.

To really appreciate the ADA, it's helpful to travel abroad sometimes. We've loved our trips to other parts of the world, but sometimes transportation and buildings that have steps, as well as sand, mountains and rocky terrain, become problems. Occasionally when we travel outside of the U.S., we've had to bring a helper along. The chair, with me in it, weighs over 300 pounds. When we reach a place where the wheels won't roll, I ride on my assistant's back—backpacking. Around the globe, disabled people's rights are at the bottom of the pile and it certainly is not fair for any of us.

But the U.S. definitely still has a long way to go to include people with disabilities.

There is new technology being developed every day and these tools could make my life much easier. The IBot wheelchair that climbs stairs and drives through sand is something that I, and Voc Rehab, cannot afford.

I'm looking past the IBot to the next big step, and I really think it's going to happen and should happen in my lifetime.

You're starting to see prototypes of cars that can fly. Some are fairly complicated but for others, basically, you take your regular car, add a propeller to the front and attach wings to the sides.

It's not the sort of thing you would take from Indiana to Switzerland, but I could see how it might be nice to take a shortcut over the cornfields if you're heading to the store for dog food.

I hope that's where we are going, to a flying wheelchair, or maybe a silent hovercraft. If there's going to be one in the next 20 years, I'll start saving my money now.

I also totally intend to have my own airplane someday. It would be so much easier and efficient to get from Tyner, Indiana, to Florida or California by simply boarding our own plane and flying there.

I've flown at the controls of a couple of planes before, unofficially. It's a matter of having the con-fidence to ask, and believe me, I'm willing to ask. So while I was in a friend's plane I ended up at the controls.

Just so you know, I've also driven a passenger train and piloted a mini sub. They're not much different from running a wheelchair or a boom truck. You learn what the levers do, and you pay attention to where you're going.

I haven't had flying lessons yet, and I probably won't get my chance until some rules are changed. As I understand it, the Federal Aviation Administration has a three-limb rule. You have to have some combination of arms and legs that add up to three if you want to be a pilot. The theory is, you need to be able to activate three controls at once. I just need to convince the FAA that three of my limbs are strong and long enough to handle the controls.

My friend Jessica Cox in Arizona has no arms and is trying to become a pilot. With all the adaptive devices that are available, there's no reason she can't handle a plane.

Then the next hurdle will be my wife, who isn't fond of flying.

If I want to sign up for flying lessons, it shouldn't be an arm-and-leg issue. I hope it will only be a husband-wife issue.

CHAPTER ELEVEN

"A good first impression is essential. People have all kinds of different ways of greeting each other. Some folks kiss. Some shake hands. Others nod or just say, "Wazzup." For me, I like a handshake. If I extend my arm, grab the end of it, just like you would someone's hand. If you meet someone new and don't know what to do, it's OK to ask them how they give a greeting. That gives us a chance to figure things out together."

— Brett Eastburn

IT NEVER OCCURRED TO ME that I might go through life as a single man. I figured I would find someone to love, marry and spend the rest of my life with. And in typical fashion, I went about finding that person in my own peculiar way. You might say I was girl crazy from the start. I met a couple girls during kindergarten and immediately claimed them as my girlfriends. In fifth grade, I scored my first kiss from Cherri Sheler.

We were boyfriend/girlfriend for a few weeks or so, and we're still friends now. One of our favorite memories is of an evening when she was pushing me in my wheelchair down a sidewalk. As we were crossing an alley, there was a car headed our way a half-block down from us. She stopped at the alley and we both saw the slow-moving car coming at us.

I screamed as if we were in immediate danger. This made her laugh to the point where she could no longer push me. I kept screaming for her to push me out of the way of the slow-moving car, which just made her laugh more. The closer the car got, the louder I screamed as if I were in real danger and the more she laughed.

The first kiss went something like this: We were sitting in my parents' old Chevy van. I asked her if I could kiss her, and she said yes. That's one of the things I've learned about women. They like you to ask.

I've never been shy about women. I've figured it's just working the odds. If you ask enough women out, someone eventually will accept. I've also figured out that it's best to be direct and honest. Sometimes you need to set the ground rules early: Are we going out on a real date, or are we just two friends going to the same movie together? The best way to find out is to ask.

I haven't been totally mature about my relationships. I was engaged twice while I was still in high school. When I found a woman I thought I could spend the rest of my life with, I would ask her to marry me. These were both women I cared about deeply at the time and still consider friends today. But I'm grateful we never got to the wedding stage because I realize now I never had the depth of love that would sustain a marriage.

After I moved to Indianapolis, I met a woman through a telephone chat room. We clicked immediately, arranged to meet and were together for about three years. We were engaged, and I thought we would get married.

When I left Essex and moved back to North Liberty, we still technically were engaged, I guess. But within a year, I thought of myself as completely single again. I wasn't particularly enjoying it.

I was starting to have some doubts. I was totally self-confident about finding women to date. At a bar or a grocery, I could easily meet an interesting woman, charm her and make her laugh. I was attractive and interesting enough, so they would want to go out and get to know me better.

At some point, though, I began to wonder. Am I just someone it was OK to date but not to marry? I started thinking about how I must look to some women. If we got married and had children together and something terrible happened, how would I protect them? Or would they spend their lives protecting me?

This self-doubt was a new experience for me. Usually, I charge into things. I find a way around everything that tries to stop me. But at age 27, I was wondering if I had reached my limit.

So it was on Oct. 23, 2000. My friend Chad Kling had called and asked me if I wanted to play pool with him at Corby's, a downtown bar in South Bend that is popular with Notre Dame students.

Chad and I have been friends for years, ever since he wrestled against me in high school. He was on the team at LaVille, one of my school's biggest rivals, and I had been forced to forfeit a match against him because I didn't reach the minimum weight.

I asked his teammates to arrange for us to wrestle anyway, in an exhibition match. When Chad showed up on the mat and saw me for the first time, he thought it was some sort of practical joke. Then, of course, "The Stub" pinned him, and we've been friends ever since.

We had a nice friendship during our 20s. We would go to a bar, play pool and try to meet girls.

On this night, I was reluctant to go. Pool wasn't the problem. I had become good enough at it that I could beat all but the best players. I just didn't want to go looking for women in a college bar. We were townies under the shadow of Notre Dame's Golden Dome. We wouldn't stand a chance with all the Domer boys.

I agreed to go, with one restriction. We wouldn't try to talk with any women in the bar. So that was the deal.

It turned out to be quite a night. We played pool, had a lot of laughs and I made eye contact with this really, really pretty blond woman. She was there with a guy, and they seemed to be having a great time. Normally, I might have said hello, just to find out more about her, but Chad and I had the agreement. No talking to women in the bar.

One of the things I do when I go to a new place is try to meet the owner. On that night at Corby's, I introduced myself to the owner, Ross. I challenged him to a game of darts, and a big crowd gathered to watch us. During the game, he threw a bull's-eye. Right after that, I threw a bull's-eye. The crowd went a little nuts when I beat him.

I had it in my head that I hoped the blond woman was watching all that, but she seemed to have left. Turns out she was watching me just as much as I was watching her.

When I say this was an unusual night, I have real evidence. There was a full moon. For some odd reason, members of the Hell's Angels motorcycle club were there. And at one point, one of the women bartenders decided to drive her new Harley into the bar, where she was doing burn-outs on the floor.

It was just a crazy, crazy night.

When it was time to leave, Chad opened the door and I had my chair revved up to about 6 miles an hour. There was no wheelchair ramp, so I basically launched myself. It wasn't quite like Evel Knievel flying over a canyon, but it created quite an impression on the people outside Corby's.

One of those people watching was the blond gal I had been tracking earlier. Since we were now outside the bar, I figured my deal with Chad was over. I rolled over to meet her.

I'm no fool. I did the proper thing. I asked the guy she was with whether they were together as a couple. As it turns out, they were just friends. If I wanted to ask her out, it was cool with him.

So I introduced myself and found out her name was Chrisa Hill; yes, she was interested in going out with me.

You need to know a little more about Chrisa.

In retrospect, I feel like we should have met somewhere before. She grew up in South Bend, about 20 miles away from me. We went to the same pediatrician. We enjoyed the same sorts of things, but as far as we know, we never saw each other before that night at Corby's.

She had gone to private schools—the Trinity School at Greenlawn and St. Joseph's High School, both in South Bend. Her goal from the time she was a toddler was to become a pediatrician.

As the math and science classes got harder, she lost the will to compete academically. She fell in with the party crowd, didn't go to a regular college and chose instead to go to a beauty college. She was working as a hair stylist when I met her.

Chrisa had a series of boyfriends, many of whom her parents didn't approve. She was in a relationship that didn't seem to be going anywhere, with a guy who seemed to be looking around for other options.

Thank heaven for her buddy, Mark Makowski III, who was with her at Corby's. Whenever Chrisa would decide that all men were no-good liars, she could hang with Mark and get her head on straight.

She wasn't planning to spend the rest of her life as a hair stylist. She had volunteered with hospitals and health agencies. Her plan was to sign up with Mother Teresa's order and move to Calcutta, India, to help in the slums. Obviously, she was not your typical Corby's gal.

On that night, she had looked across the room at Corby's and seen Chad and me playing pool. She turned to one of her friends and said, "Who's the cute guy over there with the short guy?"

They all laughed, thinking she was referring to me, the guy without the legs, as the short guy. In her view, Chad, at 5-foot-1, was the short guy. I was the cute guy.

I wish I had known that while I was sweating out asking for her number.

After I had launched myself into the street outside Corby's and introduced myself, she gave me her business card, and I told her I would call her. I also wanted to make sure she knew I was serious. I kept emphasizing it was going to be a real date.

I think she started to get a little annoyed about it, but I didn't want to get my hopes too high if she was just joking around.

Her friends told me later that I must have made a real impression on her. When she told them about me, they noticed something different about her. She must have known I wasn't one of those guys who was going to use her and break her heart.

Her friends seemed to feel something about me, too. Mark told her, "You better go out with this guy, and don't hurt him."

When she mentioned me to her father, his reaction was, "What are you bringing home now?" She had been through her fair share of dating. Her folks weren't going to tell her who to date, but they knew she hadn't been happy with her choices so far.

Her dad probably didn't realize he literally would have to carry me into their house.

I called Chrisa three days later, as promised, and arranged to pick her up at her home later that night. Our plan was to play some pool at Corby's and have dinner at Nick's Patio, a restaurant nearby.

I drove up to her house in my big wheelchair van. And, of course, her house was not wheelchair-accessible. Chrisa sent her dad out to carry me on his back into the house. It's not the way most people meet their future father-in-law for the first time, but it seemed to work for me.

I'm not licensed to give advice to the lovelorn. I can only tell you what works for me. Most men absolutely dread meeting the parents of the woman they hope to date. They'll put it off as long as they can. Me, I want to meet the parents right away. It's like meeting the owner the first time you visit a restaurant. Get comfortable with each other. With any luck, you'll be coming back.

Also, if you have any doubts about the person you're dating, you can get a lot of clues from the mom and dad. You see how they treat each other, and it tells you how your new girlfriend will expect you to act.

101

In Chrisa's case, you can tell right away that her parents have it together. They respect each other's opinions and don't raise their voices if they disagree. She's told me that she's never seen them in a yelling fight. That's about as nice a thing as you can say about a married couple.

I'll have to admit that Chrisa and I had a great time at Corby's and then settled in for the real deal-breaker part of the date. We sat at Nick's Patio and had one of the most intense, serious discussions I can ever remember having. And remember, this was just a first date.

I wanted to get all the big questions out of the way. She wanted to know, for example, whether I was born this way or whether something had happened to me. She wanted to know if I was helpless in any way, if it was going to be a lot of work taking care of me. She also wanted to know, if we ever got that far, whether we would be able to have children together. A lot of people dance around these subjects, but she didn't.

She must have liked the answers I gave her. I tell the truth and I'm sincere. But I know you take a lot of risks when you do that. A lot of people are turned off right away when you bring God into your first real conversation. Especially when you say something like this: "I was born this way because God wants me to help other people recognize their own potential."

It can sound a bit egotistical to say God has a

special plan just for you.

Chrisa tells me that was the sort of thing she had always hoped to hear. She has dreams of her own, but she always felt she wanted to be a housewife and to have a happy family. To her, a happy husband means a happy home.

In the larger sense, though, she said her mission in life would be to help lift people up. That's why she had been thinking about dedicating her life to Mother Teresa's work. She saw what I was doing for a living, with my speaking career, and she saw it as something she could support. We just clicked.

I have this theory about relationships. I believe you need two real/full halves to make a whole. Each person needs to have a lot of their issues worked out in advance so they're ready to meet the person that will make them whole.

I've told you about my struggles, about my successes and failures, about my family and friends, about my personal insecurities. I have had a happy life, generally, but I had to learn about unhappiness. I've had companionship, but I had to learn about loneliness.

Chrisa and I, from the first date onward, have not hidden from our pasts. She's met many of the women I knew before her. I'm grateful for the men that came before me in Chrisa's life. I think they helped prepare her for someone who would love her as much as I do.

A few days after we met, we both had Halloween

parties to attend with people that we had been dating. We didn't talk about it in advance, but I broke up with my longtime girlfriend in Indianapolis that night and she broke up with her on-and-off boyfriend.

I knew Chrisa was different from the women I had met before. And it scared me a bit.

I felt I knew everything about her. But there was one thing no one told me about. Chrisa had a birthday coming up on Nov. 10. She says, for as long as she can remember, she had been telling her parents about how much she loves roses. The first man who buys me a dozen roses, she said, is the man I'm going to marry.

On her 24th birthday, she was at work at the hair salon. A big box showed up, and her friends all wondered about it. Her name was on it. When she opened the box, she saw it was from me. Inside were a dozen red roses.

She told her friends: "Oh, my God, I'm going to marry this man."

I was at her house later that day, and the subject of the dozen roses came up. Her parents let me know how much of an impression I had made.

I told them that, sadly, I would be able to give their daughter a dozen roses only once more. And they gave me a worried look, wondering if there was some problem.

"Well," I said, "they cost me an arm and a leg."

CHAPTER TWELVE

"Two of the most powerful words are 'thank you.' Too often, we're surprised by a sincere compliment and act like we don't deserve anyone's praise. When you say 'thank you,' you're telling the other person their words are appreciated and you're telling yourself subconsciously that maybe they're right."

— Brett Eastburn

CHRISA AND I HAD LITTLE DOUBT of our future together. We talked about marriage right away. After just a month, when I let those three dangerous words slip—I love you—I meant them.

Fortunately, Chrisa felt the same way about me. And so did her parents. They told her, "If you dump this one, we're keeping him and losing you."

We were engaged a couple months later and married on May 27, 2000. We're both a little math-challenged and we easily forget dates. So getting married in the year 2000 has been great for both of us. Easy math to figure out how many years we've been married.

Was I nervous about getting married? Well, I'm physically exempt from getting cold feet. But I'll have to admit I went through a period where the thought of a lifetime commitment scared me.

I'm an independent guy. Over the years, I had gotten used to fighting my own battles and taking the lumps when things didn't work out right. My career hadn't taken off as well as I wanted, and I knew my life wasn't going to be perfect. I wanted badly, for Chrisa's sake, to be able to have the type of life together she deserved.

As much as I like to look on the bright side, I didn't have a clear path to get where I wanted to go.

That's where I learned one of the most important lessons of my life. No matter how independent you are, if you're going into a relationship of any sort, you need to learn to rely on the other person.

Part of it is compromise. If you want or need different things, sometimes you need to talk it through and figure out whose needs should be served first. But just as important, we have to learn to accept help. It's not a sign of weakness in me if you offer a hand and I accept it.

We had been dating a couple months before Chrisa finally got a chance to see one of my speeches. She accompanied me to an elementary school, where I gave what I thought was one of my typical talks.

When I saw her afterward, she was in tears. She had heard me say almost all the same words before, but she was a bit overwhelmed when she saw how I put it all together.

"You need to stop fooling around with those other jobs and do this full time," she said. And she told me she would quit her job and help, too.

That, basically, was the beginning of No Boundaries Inc., the business she and I continue to run today. She knew I could talk a good talk but I didn't have the money sense to make a business work. She also knew that running a business was part of her genetic code. She calls it her family finesse. Her father and grandfather both were expert salesmen, and she figured that was what No Boundaries needed most.

We started putting the pieces of this business together at the same time we were planning our wedding. A friend and I designed a brochure and we were committed to mailing thousands of them out to schools, businesses and organizations that were likely to hire speakers like me.

Our families thought we had lost our minds. The timing was strange, not just because we were five months away from a wedding. Our mailing date was going to be my birthday, Dec. 28, 1999.

In hindsight, the Y2K scare is something of a joke. People were worried then that, on the stroke of midnight as the new millennium started, every computer in the world would crash. That was because computer systems were said to be set up with the first two digits of the year fixed at 19. So when 2000 started, the computers would read it as 1900 instead.

I'm no smarter than anyone else. If the computer systems all crashed and worldwide chaos ensued, I wanted to be prepared, too. I went out to the grocery store and bought a few of the 24 packs of toilet paper. I didn't want to be caught short if the economic panic caused a run on toilet paper.

But I was determined that, Y2K or not, the world would need to listen to what I have to say. I couldn't get a loan from the bank to start my business, so a family member loaned us the money to mail our brochures. We had it figured out that we could pay the loan back if we were hired by just one of every 200 organizations we contacted.

We had total faith that it would work out. Instead of that expected 0.5 percent return, ours was about 3 percent. So here we were, already exceeding our dreams.

It would be nice to say that things just kept getting better and better for us. In some ways they have. But life isn't supposed to be easy, and it wasn't for us.

For one, we had planned to start our new life together in a brand-new apartment in Lakeville, a small town down the road from North Liberty. We had signed our lease six months in advance, when the apartments were under construction. We told the apartment managers of our deadline, and we were assured the work would be done on time.

It wasn't. There was a problem with getting approved for handicap access. So we ended up spending the first three months of our married life with my parents. We both love my parents, but I wouldn't advise anyone to have that sort of arrangement.

During those first few weeks, a lot of crucial decisions are made. You're going from that stage of courtship where you're trying to put your best foot forward, to the everyday life, where sometimes things get a little twisted up and awkward.

You want to work out your routines on your own. It's a little difficult to do that when you know your parents are within earshot. Whether they want to be or not, they are part of your conversations. Still, it's an example of family and friends being there for us, helping us get our start.

At that same time, we were starting our business, getting ready to move into our new apartment and buying a motorhome that would take us to my speaking engagements. It was hard to keep up with everything that was going on around me.

In my view, we benefited from the chaos. People who have things easy have no reason to push for change. You get comfortable. You stop thinking and dreaming. The chaos makes you move. Out of chaos comes success.

I figure we were lucky. With all these things going on around us, we had to make a special effort to think about our relationship. We knew we loved each other, and we knew we had a friendship that would grow stronger with time. We also had God at the center of our lives. When we needed guidance, we could pray. We didn't have to come up with every answer ourselves.

Some people asked if we weren't taking on a big risk, starting our own business at such an early age and so early into our marriage. In our view, we needed to hurry to make up for lost time. I was 27 already and Chrisa was 24. We both felt we should have been further along in our careers by then.

It can be difficult to work with your spouse, especially when one person takes the starring role and the other serves as support. I'm not perfect, but I've tried to think of Chrisa as a 50 percent partner in the business. She's the one who gets the bookings and makes all the arrangements. Without her, I would have nowhere to go and no way to get there.

Realistically, if I worked hard enough on preparations, I could go anywhere in the world without her. It would be hard. I would have to think through each step of the trip, figuring out what I would do if the simplest things went wrong. If I absolutely had to, I could do it.

The problem, though, is I wouldn't enjoy it. I would be so preoccupied with the details that I couldn't notice the good things happening around me. I treasure having Chrisa to enjoy moments with. When we were in Switzerland together, I would see something totally beautiful, like a mirror pool. I want to be able to ask her right away, "Do you see what I see?" A text message or a camera phone just aren't enough.

But there have been times when each of us has had to stop being spouses and look at ourselves as business partners. You just say what needs to be said. I had already been making speeches professionally for eight years before I met her. Sometimes when she would ask me why I was doing things a certain way, I just had to say, "Don't worry about it. Trust me. I don't have an answer right now." And that's truly what it takes. Trust. Faith. And another thing: Patience.

I am grateful she's with me at almost all my speeches. I'm susceptible to panic attacks. Sometimes, I'll get so anxious before a speech that I just don't want to go on. I'm afraid I'll get halfway into it and forget what I'm supposed to say next. It's just an unreasonable fear that creeps in. The odd thing about it is, it rarely happens before a speech in a new town or a foreign country.

My worst panic attack came before a speech to the local Chamber of Commerce. I knew almost everyone in the room. I had given the speech thousands of times before. But somehow, I had this overpowering sense of dread. I begged Chrisa to give the speech for me. Even though she declined, I was so grateful to have her with me. She knows about my fear and knows how to talk me through it.

Our goal, together, was to create a program that would work for all ages and all occasions. Clients would call and ask for something specific, like a message on diversity, tolerance or some other issue. When I would show up, I would give the same speech I gave everywhere else, and they would be thrilled. Diversity is in that speech. So is tolerance. So are striving for success, and overcoming obstacles, and all the other things people need to hear to be a self-advocate.

Another goal was to have a business that we could operate from anywhere. We didn't want to have to be in a big city, like Chicago or Orlando or Washington, D.C. In fact, when we started looking around, we decided to move from little North Liberty into an even smaller town.

My friend Dave Brooke lives in Tyner, a cluster of homes way out in the country. To get to his house, you drive past a bunch of cornfields, cross a railroad track, follow a big bend in the road and turn right into a gravel driveway. He's been my best friend since second grade; so we were driving down to see him a couple times a week.

One day, we noticed the house next door was for sale. Chrisa was a city girl. She was used to being two minutes away from the mall, two minutes from work, two minutes from the grocery, two minutes from school.

When I suggested moving to Tyner, she wanted to know what you do at 10 p.m. when you're out of milk. Folks in Tyner know the answer. You either plan ahead or you go without. She's found out that small towns offer the best of life. You have close neighbors who know you well enough to mind their own business.

To us, everyone in Tyner is family. Neighborhood kids wander in and out of our house. If someone's shower is broken or if their refrigerator is on the blink, they know they're welcome to use ours until they figure out how to get the thing fixed.

North Liberty is just up the road a ways, and one of the blessings of staying near your hometown is that you keep in touch with the people who helped you grow up. Whenever I go into a store or restaurant, I run into people who know me well enough to have stories to tell.

We have lunch from time to time at places like the American Legion Hall in North Liberty. The food's great, but the real reason to go is to see old neighbors. It seems like we know everyone there. And on a recent trip we ran into Roger Lawson.

Roger is one of those guys who always seemed to be around me when I was growing up, and he's a natural storyteller. He tells me things I had forgotten, like the time someone asked me how I lost my legs. My answer? "If I had really lost them, I would have by-God found them by now."

He remembers how, when I would go on a first date, I would have reassuring words for the fathers of the girls I was taking out. "Don't worry," I would say. "I won't lay a hand on her."

There were other little practical jokes I would pull at school. Sometimes we would have a carload of kids going to wrestling practice. I would wait until we were almost out of my driveway and then tell one of the guys I had forgotten my shoes. He would go running into the house looking for them. It usually took a while for the guy to realize I was pulling his leg.

One time at school, I was almost out of the classroom when the teacher realized the joke was on him. He had given me a hall pass so I could go fetch my gloves out of my locker.

One recent time when I saw Roger, he started talking about Charley, an old horse he had. He would let us take Charley down to the creek, where we would crawl up on the horse's back and use him as a diving platform. One day, as we were getting ready to take Charley out, I was giving Roger some sass, and he threatened to wash my mouth out with soap.

I didn't think he could do it. But while I wasn't looking, he put soap on Charley's reins. He knew the way I would drive Charley was to put his reins in my mouth. So that's how he got me.

That's one of those stories I had forgotten.

Chrisa and I have talked about having children of our own. It's a topic a lot of people have asked us about. Sometimes they're careful about asking it, but the question will end up being, "Are you afraid your children will end up looking like you?"

Think about that for a while. You can imagine how insulting that sounds.

The answer is, no, we're not afraid. We don't

know if whatever happened to me would happen to any children we have. I'm guessing it wouldn't, but I haven't taken any genetic tests to find out for sure.

The real answer, though, is that we're not afraid because being like me is pretty darn cool. If we had a child with no arms or legs, I have all the problems worked out. I could teach Brett Jr. or Chrisa Jr. how to throw a football, play pool, fish, eat soup or do any of the thousands of things I had to learn for myself.

If I passed along the genetics, I also would be passing along the knowledge. That child would have a big head start on the rest of the world.

I find it strange how helpless some people think I am. Even after my speeches, where I've broken a karate board and told stories about all the things I've done, people come up to Chrisa and tell her how proud they are of her.

She must be some kind of saint to devote herself to a person who can do so little for himself. Maybe they've listened to the speech, but they've totally missed the point.

A lot of people with disabilities are sensitive about the vocabulary people use around them. They don't like to be called a "person in a wheelchair." The reason for that is, it puts the emphasis on the chair, not the person. It's like choosing a winner in the Kentucky Derby. You pick the horse, and you think the jockey is just the little guy along for the ride. Or choosing the car to win the Indianapolis 500 and not recognizing the driver. That's insulting, don't you think?

The same goes for "person in a wheelchair." It's like the chair is the main character, and I'm just the guy who happens to be sitting there. Just a small change makes a lot of difference. Call it a "person using a wheelchair" and it gives a better sense of the reality, which is: I'm a regular guy who's in charge of the chair.

I pay attention to what I hear, but I try not to be ultra-sensitive about it. If you say it wrong, I might correct you or I might let it pass. It depends on whether I think you've had a slip of the tongue or whether I think you need to have your awareness improved.

In any case, I'm not going to bark at you. If I want you to have a better understanding of people using wheelchairs, I don't want you to think we all are short-tempered, too.

Still, I might hear things differently from the way you do.

For example, when anyone goes into a restaurant or a store, it's common for the greeter to say, "May I help you?" or "How may I help you?"

That is what they're trained to say. They say it to everyone who comes in the door. To a person in a wheelchair, the word "help" is sometimes heard the wrong way. Because they are in a chair, maybe people think they are helpless. The greeter or waitress might

117

be looking at them and assuming, because of their circumstances, they need special attention.

If I had my way, you would say, "If there is anything you need, please let me know." A majority of the disabled community would take this statement as a bit more non-threatening.

I lived for several years on my own before I met Chrisa. All the things she does for me now are things I was able to do for myself before I met her. I know all about the "Start" button on the microwave.

I agree, she is some kind of a saint. But it's not because she cuts up my food or does my laundry. She is a saint because she treats everyone well, even the ignorant people who think she is sacrificing so much to be with me.

The answer to the obviously nosy question, why we haven't had children, is the same one a lot of young professionals have. We don't have the time yet to be the kind of parents we would want to be.

I know some people are great parents, even though they're on the road 200 days a year. They come up with some sort of arrangement where one parent or the other puts in the extra at-home time.

In our case, Chrisa and I both are out of the house at the same time. We're both road people. She goes where I go. We could take a child with us for the first few years, but we're planning on doing this long after any child of ours would reach school age. Ideally, we could have children of our own to raise, but we don't want to be absentee parents.

We love children, and in some ways we think that's why we love Tyner and our career so much. Even after I make my million dollars, I'll still live here and still travel, educate and entertain. We truly believe that it takes a village to raise a child. We're doing our best to be part of that village.

The way Chrisa approaches it is, she expects to have a conversation with God someday in heaven. God will tell her that he had placed a child in her path. He will want to know what we did about it.

Her view is, we see thousands of children each year. We are responsible for the influence we have on each child that crosses our path.

We need to be able to say we loved them and we helped them. All children. Even those we see only once.

We love to travel. I had a chance to go to Switzerland a couple years ago.

You're never really sure how these things happen, but I think the person who invited me had seen my comedy routine on YouTube. He called and asked if we could be there in two weeks. As luck would have it, we had just received our passports for another trip we had planned, so we took a chance on a spur-of-the-moment offer.

I knew very little about the event, except that they were paying all my expenses for a four-day trip and all they wanted was a 10-minute presentation. It was called the Swiss Economic Forum, and one of the other speakers was former New York City mayor Rudy Giuliani. A former Olympic medalist swimmer, John Naber, was there too.

I figured while I was there I would try out a comedy club. It turns out Switzerland is a really serious place. You can tell. Everything there looks like it was done with great purpose and sincerity. Even the cows. They're huge and they look happy.

But there were no comedy clubs in the whole country.

I've been to Aruba twice. In fact, it's the only place in the world where I am big-time famous.

The last time we went, there were news crews at the airport meeting our plane. I looked around, expecting to see Tom Cruise or some big celebrity there. But as it turns out, they were all there to see me.

I'm not sure why it happened like that. But somehow, I became the biggest news of the day. It's an island with 90,000 people, and it has five newspapers, three radio stations and two local TV channels. I was interviewed by every one of them.

The Aruba version of Oprah, at the time, was a woman named Deka. I was on her show too. And every day we were there, we were swarmed by people who recognized us from being on TV or in the newspapers.

We went to a fast-food restaurant, a Taco Bell, and everyone wanted me to sign autographs on napkins. We would go other places, and entire kitchen staffs would want to come out and meet me.

I got away from the hubbub one day and went to shoot pool in a cantina. While I was playing, a girl who was watching called her dad, who showed up on his Harley and insisted we come to his restaurant. It was called the Amazonia, and it had the best salad bar I've ever seen. But you would make a mistake filling up on salad. Every couple of minutes, waiters would come by with all kinds of meat—beef, pork, chicken, shellfish, everything. He wouldn't let us pay anything for dinner.

I'll have to admit I put in a lot of time to earn my fame. We were busy with programs and interviews from 7 a.m. to 8 p.m. every day. That was the price of being the Hasselhof of Aruba.

CHAPTER THIRTEEN

"There's a fine line between laughing at your situation and making fun of yourself to receive negative attention. It's like a card game. Sometimes you're dealt a bad hand. If you enjoy the game, you don't mind losing once in a while. That's part of the joy of living. But if you tear yourself down when you lose, the game's no fun. Laugh with life, not at it." — Brett Eastburn

I'VE ALWAYS BEEN ABLE TO make people laugh. I'm not totally sure why. I know, on some levels, I use humor to make people comfortable with me. And, believe me, that's important.

If you're having a typical day, the last thing you expect to see is a guy with no arms and legs. It's a shock. I've seen the looks on people's faces when they meet me for the first time. You wonder if they're going to run away and hide.

If I have something funny to say, it can put them at ease. The next thing you know, they're not looking at me, wondering where my arms and legs are. Instead, they're listening, wondering what I'm going to say next.

I love a good sight gag, too.

There was the time back in middle school when I took a girl on a date to the bowling alley. She wanted a pop, so I went over to the vending machine, put the coins in and pressed a button. The pop can dropped into the deep tray at the bottom of the machine. I jumped out of my chair and reached into the machine to root around for the can.

At that moment, a kid walked by and saw my arm deep into that low tray. He looked really confused by it. So I started screaming bloody murder. By his reaction, I think I had him believing that the machine was eating me. He started running in circles with his arms flailing around high in the air worried that I was trapped and then he ran into the other room yelling HELP! HELP!

For years, I've included humor in my public speeches. It's almost required. If you start a speech with a sad story or a serious observation, your audience is almost certain to start looking at their watches. They know they're in for an hour of hard listening. Most people want to be informed and enlightened, but they mainly want to be entertained. A good joke or two will get them on your side.

A real laugh breaks the ice. It can make them forget that they're sitting there in a suit, surrounded by other people wearing suits. They lose that sense of being locked up in a room, unable to go out and play. And physically, laughter causes your body to release endorphins, which help you relax.

I always figured, at some point, I would become a successful standup comedian in addition to the public speaking. I didn't realize then how difficult comedy is. It's really hard work to get other people to have fun.

I attended my first comedy workshops when I was living in Indianapolis. We had a small group of people who would try out jokes on each other. We would talk about what makes a joke funny. Then we would go back and rewrite our jokes and try it all over again.

One of the first things you learn is that there's a huge difference between being "cute" and being funny. Some of us would start out with cute little stories that made the others smile. That's not nearly enough. You need to get real laughs and they have to come often.

If you're talking for five minutes, you want your audience to be laughing about 30 percent of the time.

You also learn early on that it's really dangerous for a comedian to try to tell a long story. An audience doesn't want to sit and listen. They want to laugh. And if you make them wait too long for a punch line, sometimes they forget what it's like to laugh. You might pull off a story joke, but you need to plant little laugh lines along the way.

I also learned that the stage is a completely different place for comics. I've known people who were able to tell a joke around the campfire that is so good that everyone loses it. Then when they try to tell it onstage, it doesn't work. They spend the next three years tinkering with it, trying to get it to translate to real comedy.

I didn't know any of that when I started the workshops. I figured I always had ways of making my friends laugh. So I should be able to just get up on the stage, act like everyone in the audience was a buddy from North Liberty, and I would be on my way.

If that were true, a lot of people would be knocking their audiences dead every time a bar has an open-mic night. The truth is, very few people are naturally funny enough to be onstage. Maybe one guy in a million gets it right away, the first time up.

Most guys are like Larry the Cable Guy, who was

doing comedy for 20 years before he finally came up with an act that works. Same thing with another funny guy, Lewis Black. He stood in front of a lot of quiet audiences before he finally hit it big.

That's because a comedian really doesn't get to be himself too often. You have to find a different voice that is going to connect with people in the comedy clubs. Are you going to be angry or sarcastic or a real doofus? Which part of your character is going to work?

Then there's all that stuff about stage management. Are you holding the microphone correctly? What do you do with the stand when you take the mic into your hand? Do you stand straight up or slump? Are you still or do you pace the stage? Can your audience hear you? Do you waste your best lines because they're still laughing and miss the zinger?

I got my first chance in front of a live audience in Indianapolis. I had three or four minutes of material. Some of the jokes I told that night are still in the show I use nearly two decades later. I got enough laughs that I didn't feel like a complete fool, but I knew I had a lot more work to do. If I was going to be a comedian, I was going to have to expand my act and push my limits.

Frankly, I didn't have the time then to work on it. When I moved back to North Liberty, I was busy with regular jobs. Then I got married, bought a house, bought a motor home and started my own business. To make it all work, I needed to be doing about 200 speeches a year. If I had the time, I didn't have the energy to be really funny. So I kept putting it off.

One of the benefits of my job is that I meet a lot of people. Some of them really connect with me and we become close friends. Dave Harrison, who runs a trucking company in Illinois, is one of those guys. We had been talking once a week for about 15 years, me encouraging him and him encouraging me. One day, he finally said to me, "It's time for you to go back to comedy."

I think I was a little scared by that. I had been willing to rest on my laurels, having made a few strangers laugh in Indianapolis a long time ago. I had not failed as a comedian. I had just tried it, enjoyed it and left it behind.

But what Dave said made me realize I had violated one of my biggest rules. I believe in striving for success. If you try something once and fail, go back and do it again, a thousand times if necessary, until you master it. That's the only way I've been able to accomplish the things I've done so far in my life.

But persistence can be your enemy once you become successful. No great work has been achieved by someone doing the same thing the same way a thousand times. Greatness comes only when you have that lump in your throat because you're trying something new. You improvise. You stretch. And from your struggles will come something that is uniquely you.

I had become successful as a speaker. I wasn't improvising or stretching the way I used to.

Part of me wanted to tell Dave to mind his own business. After all, I wasn't telling him how to run his trucks. But the part of me that makes me special is the part that says, "I can do that." Dave knows that. He knew I needed a push.

I found a comedy workshop in Mishawaka, about 20 minutes from my home. There, with the help of some really funny guys, I started putting together another comedy act.

I thought it would be easier this time. After all, I had about two decades of experience speaking in front of audiences large and small. I had solved a lot of the stage management issues. I had learned a lot about the sort of voice the audience wanted from a guy like me. All I would need to do is to write a "handful" of new jokes.

As it turns out, my years as a public speaker were a mixed blessing. Sure, I had the confidence and techniques. But I had to un-learn a lot of what I had been doing. When I first returned to comedy, my bits sounded too much like speeches. In a speech, you might spend an hour telling stories, building up to a great one-liner at the finish. In comedy, you need to forget about the one-hour story. You just zing in with the one-liner.

After two months of workshops, I was really beginning to feel confident. I was polishing a little three-minute set. I had performed it in front of my friends and some local comedians. It had been critiqued and reworked and critiqued again. I figured I would keep working on it until it was ready.

I didn't know it, but one of my comic friends, John Osborn, had gone to the manager of the Funny Bone club and told him I was ready. So one night I was there to see someone else's show. John didn't tell me I was going to perform until about five minutes before I was introduced.

It was a frantic five minutes as I tried to reorganize my jokes. Finally, ready or not, my name was called.

The first thing I noticed was that I couldn't get up on the stage. My wheelchair couldn't go up the steps. Eventually, I made my entrance by hopping up on a table. If I had been nervous about public speaking before, my first night at the Funny Bone took it to a completely different level. I was so nervous that my scalp went numb.

One of the comedian tricks is that you ask if people

are having fun. That gets them clapping or hooting or whatever. So that's what I did. Then I said, "I would give you a thumbs-up, but I might hurt myself."

That earned me my first laugh. It also addressed the discomfort some in the audience might have with my physical appearance. I was going to joke about myself. They were going to laugh. That was settled.

As far as laughter goes, I'm not too picky about it. There are all kinds of laughs, and I appreciate every one of them. What I don't want is silence. If people sit and give you that blank stare, it's the worst feeling in the world.

I've worked on pacing my performance. If I have just three minutes, I have to make sure I have the punch lines coming fast and furious. If I have five minutes, I have a little more time to make connections with the audience. But if you ever become the star attraction, you might have a whole hour.

In my opinion, it's almost easier when you have the whole hour. You don't have to condense each joke into a one-liner, looking for ways to deliver it quickly so you can pack more stuff into your three minutes. The more time you have, the better your chances of just being yourself.

I figure comedy is a lot like playing pool. You can't go into it hoping to win. You have to believe in your abilities and expect to come out on top.

It helps to have a fellow comedian in your corner, too. Sometimes when I'm not so certain about myself, John Osborn will say to me, "Stop worrying about it and be funny."

When he says it, it sounds like an easy thing to do.

CHAPTER FOURTEEN

"We are not here to judge others. You can't judge someone unless you know everything about them. And unless you can read minds, you'll never be able to do that. I believe there is a final judge for all of us. I'll let His decision stand."

— Brett Eastburn

ONE OF MY EARLIEST MEMORIES is from my church. I was lying in my mother's lap, falling asleep while she stroked my ear. In some ways, that's what I still get

133

out of church all these years later—comfort, support and love.

My grandfather—my father's father—was a pastor in Fairmount, Indiana, so it makes sense that we were a church-going family. My first home was just a mile away from the North Liberty Church of Christ. We went nearly every Sunday.

A story they tell about me was that one Sunday I was sitting in the church nursery, next to some dolls. An older girl walked in and saw me, thinking I was a broken doll with no arms and legs. As she came over to play with me, I moved. It scared the tar out of her.

I remember enjoying church because my friends and family were there. But I also enjoyed hearing stories from the Bible. My favorite was about David and Goliath. Since I was born so small, it wasn't difficult for me to imagine being David and having to come up with a special strategy to defeat the giant.

I received a lot of good advice from listening to those stories and to the pastors who told them. In some churches, you're baptized soon after you're born. In ours, they leave it up to you. Baptism is a conscious choice. You decide when you are ready.

I think I surprised my mom when I was 12 years old and I chose to be baptized on Mother's Day. I thought of it as a gift to her, but it was a gift to myself, too.

My wife grew up in the People of Praise, and the Catholic Church. She describes her church experience as "spirit-filled" and "charismatic." Her parents were Eucharistic ministers, which pulled Chrisa even more deeply into the faith. She was baptized soon after birth and began living a Christ-centered life much earlier than I did.

One of the church experiences she talks about is her CCD classes—Confraternity of Christian Doctrine. Those were classes she took when she became old enough to learn about the basic Catholic beliefs. As part of that program, she attended services at a Jewish temple, a Muslim mosque and in Protestant churches. The idea was that she should know enough about other religions so she could make an informed choice.

Over the years, I've had a chance to attend some other churches, too, but I'm a bit jealous of the CCD opportunity Chrisa had. She believes the experience has made her more open and understanding. So many of us are ignorant and suspicious of the other religions. We feel we have all the answers so the other people must be wrong.

I've tried out denominations other than my home church, the Church of Christ. When I'm lucky, I find ideas that help answer questions I struggle with. Having access to all these different churches is like having dozens of tutors around when I get stuck on a tough problem.

There's a joke I heard, and I hope it doesn't offend my Catholic friends:

A Protestant dies and goes to heaven, where he meets God.

God is showing the guy all the neat stuff in heaven, and everything is full of joy. But wherever they turn, there's this tall white wall. And whenever the Protestant guy gets close to the wall, he can hear people laughing and having a good time on the other side.

So finally, he works up the courage to ask God, "I just need to know: What's on the other side of the wall and what is all that noise?"

God says, "Oh, that's just the Catholics. They think they're the only ones up here."

The reason the joke works is that you could reverse the names and the truth holds up. I meet a lot of people—Baptists, Lutherans, Methodists, Catholics, Protestants of all sorts—who feel their group has the only right answers. They seem to view heaven as a fairly small space where only a perfect score qualifies.

I certainly don't know what heaven will be like and I've never had a peek at the invitation list. Over the years, as I've met more people whose life experiences aren't like mine, my ideas have changed.

The main thing is, I hope all of us have a chance for an eternal life. I believe there isn't just one gate into heaven, and I sure hope there aren't a lot of walls when I get there.

I've spoken in a lot of churches over the years. Typically, I give the same sort of speech I would give in a school or at a business conference. A couple of times, people have come up afterward to tell me I should mention God more often. I recognize that they're trying to be helpful, but I'm not likely to change.

In my view, religion isn't much different from marshmallows. You have this wonderful thing that almost everyone seems willing to accept and enjoy. Then you start force-feeding people. Marshmallow after marshmallow, there's no letup. Eventually, you start hating the things.

No one wants religion, or marshmallows, crammed down their throats.

Chrisa and I, raised in different churches, have taken different paths but have come to the same conclusion. Faith is in all of us, in some form or another. The House of God is not a building and it doesn't have a set of rules posted on the door. It's something that grows within each of us, and it takes root in our bodies and our souls.

We still attend church on occasion and feel comfortable and loved there. In return, we love being part of congregations. They help remind us of how we developed our faith and it helps us to be part of that ongoing search for truth. Sometimes we're Catholics.

Sometimes we're Protestants. But at all times, we're believers in a better place.

I think I first became a committed Christian through an event that has nothing to do with a church.

It happened when I was in junior high school. An adult friend of mine told me that his elderly mother had fallen and broken her hip. She then had to go through a difficult surgery, but a key part of the recovery is to simply get back on your feet. The pain never goes away until you start living a normal life again.

The mother refused to try walking on her sore hip. The pain was too great for her. She was convinced that she would spend the rest of her life in a hospital bed.

It was devastating for my friend to hear his mother say that. So he started talking to her about me. He told her how I had been given a tougher challenge than she had. I had no arms or legs, but I had decided not to give up on the good things life has to offer. I was hopping around, chasing my dreams, refusing to give up on anything.

You, the son told his mother, are lying here crying about a sore hip while Brett Eastburn is out there having a blast.

The next day, she got out of bed and started walking. And that sore hip never slowed her down again.

If that story changed his mother's life, it had an even stronger effect on me. As you can imagine, as a teenager, I had been questioning a lot of what I had heard in church and Sunday School. The Bible says that God created man in his own image. So here I was, looking around at all the people with two arms and two legs. If God created me too, why would he make me the way I am?

Was I a mistake?

With this friend's help, I finally solved the riddle. I had my purpose in life. God had taken great care in creating me. He didn't just give me this unique, attention-getting body. He also gave me the willpower, the knowledge and the stamina to help myself.

In exchange, he also gave me a job. I was to show others that there are challenges God can give you that may seem impossible. But he also gives you the tools you need to face and conquer those problems.

I had found my calling.

It humbles me today to realize I had never actually spoken to my friend's mother. I didn't mix a magic potion for her. I didn't lay my hands on her and invoke God's name in seeking a miraculous healing. Nor did God give me the brainpower to become a surgeon or a medical researcher.

My story alone, just as I am, was enough to inspire someone to use her own powers to make her life better.

Over the years, I have realized that my role is supposed to be limited. I am not a preacher or a teacher. I'm not a counselor, and I'm not a parent. I'm not a constant presence in your life.

I don't know if there is a perfect word to encapsulate what it is that happens. I change others around me and the effect that they have on me is the same. We all grow and change together.

You've probably heard of John Chapman. He wandered around Ohio, Indiana and Illinois in the early 1800s, planting apple seeds wherever he went. He didn't stick around to water the seeds, pull weeds or prune the branches. He let Mother Nature take care of that.

He would come back from time to time to inspect his work, but his purpose wasn't to sell the apples from those trees. He planted. Others harvested. That's how he became known as Johnny Appleseed.

That's one of the ways I like to think of myself.

If you're old enough to remember black-and-white TV, you can think of me also as "The Lone Ranger." I can step into your life and help you solve a problem or two, and then I need to be gone so you can go to work. It may even take a year or more for the idea to take hold, and you may have forgotten everything about me.

Ideally, you'll be like the folks on the TV show, wondering, "Who was that masked man?"

I bring one piece of the puzzle. The rest is up to

you. You have all the other pieces and you arrange them however you can. You need to discover why you are on this Earth. I know why I am here, but I can't tell you for certain why you are.

There are a lot of people out there who are doing what I am doing. A lot of them will tell you about why they have become so successful. They've started out with nothing, developed their talents and battled their way to the top.

I love a good success story. But I also want you to know about failures.

I can respect the superstars, the people who somehow have taken a straight-line route to the top. Good for them. My route hasn't been a straight line at all.

I struggled in school. Maybe it was dyslexia. Maybe I was lazy. Maybe I was being rebellious or just being a class clown to get attention.

I struggled with bed-wetting well into my school years. It was humiliating for me and, again, I'm not sure I understand why it happened. Maybe, as the doctor suggested, I slept too deeply and couldn't wake myself up to use the bathroom. Maybe it was a self-esteem thing where I caused myself to fail. Nevertheless I overcame bedwetting and moved on to the next challenge.

I still struggle with anxiety attacks. I've never

failed to deliver one of my speeches. Even when I've had the flu, I've been able to summon up the energy to get through my one-hour program. Yet, many times when I'm on my way to a speech, I'm overcome with a sense of dread.

My mind goes to the dark places where doubt lurks. Maybe this will be the time my brain fails, I forget the script and my audience stares at me like I'm some sort of sideshow freak.

I can tell you about all the obstacles I've overcome. I can bounce across a stage, throw you a football and make you laugh. But I also need to tell you that I, like you, have a lot more work to do. For every challenge I meet and conquer, another one arises, sometimes bigger than before. And the satisfaction I feel multiplies as I go to work on each step.

I am not going to tell you how to have a perfect life and how to accomplish all your dreams. I don't know. I can't do it myself.

Life is good because it's difficult at times. You could take the easy way and hope someone else makes your decisions for you and knocks all of your obstacles aside. That's the way my life could have turned out. But when I was a seemingly helpless infant, my mom saw that I could learn to grip things, if she rolled my sleeves up for me. From that point on, I worked on learning even more things.

The most important thing I learned was that these things all have a purpose. And this is what I truly believe: God put me on this Earth the way I am to help inspire other people to make the absolute most of their talents and their time.

God is there, rolling up the sleeves for you and me.

If I use his help, and if you use his help, we can reach for the lives we want. We won't be missing anything.

CHAPTER FIFTEEN

WHEN I STARTED THIS BOOK, I didn't want to make it totally about myself. If I'm proud about what I've accomplished, that's cool. But why should you care? Why would you read about my successes and failures?

For me, it all boils down to this: Despite all our differences, at our very core, we are pretty much the same. I've realized over the years that there's been no one exactly like me in the history of the world. I've had no identical twin. No one else has been where I've been and experienced exactly what I've done.

But ultimately, we're all filled with the same piano keys. One key makes the happiness sound. Another sounds like sadness. There's love and hate. Fear. Joy. Boredom. Doubt. All these keys go together in different ways to form different chords. We play them differently and that's what makes us unique.

But at the most basic level, your "fear" key and mine are the same. Put the president of the United States and a comedian from Tyner, Indiana, in a car and push us over a cliff, and we likely will have the same scream. Tell us both a good joke and we'll have the same laugh.

That's the reason I wanted you to read this book. I want you to know I'm not that much different from you and we can learn from each other.

I've told you a lot of stories about myself. I hope they've illustrated some of the lessons I've learned so far.

I'll sum up those lessons here:

1. *When you say, "I can't," you will always be right. You've decided you aren't going to try.*

You've probably read that famous quote from hockey legend Wayne Gretzky, who said, "You're always going to miss 100 percent of the shots you don't take."

My biggest mission in life is to help people erase the words "I can't" from their vocabulary. If you try it once and fail, it's OK to say "I didn't," but until you've tried every possible strategy, there's always hope.

2. *In baseball, you're out after three strikes. But in life, you can keep swinging, a thousand times or more, if you really want to hit a home run. You're only out when you stop swinging.*

I'm not impressed when someone says they've given a 110 percent effort to a project. Trying hard isn't as important as trying often. If you've ever watched a squirrel trying to raid a bird feeder, you know what I mean. If you want the sunflower seed, it doesn't help if you grunt and strain extra hard each time you leap. It's better if you go at it from every possible angle until you succeed.

3. *If you can draw a circle and a straight line, you can be an artist. It's just a matter of shaping the circle differently or angling the line a little. The same thing goes for most other things you think you can't do. Break it down into simpler tasks. You'll be surprised at how easy it becomes.*

The secret to conquering a new skill is to figure out how it's similar to something you already can do. You simply build on what you already know.

The first time I was able to pick up a stuffed bunny set me up for being able to catch and throw a ball. The first time I was able to pull on a ribbon set me up for being able to dial a cell phone.

147

I hear people say all the time that they can't draw or they can't dance. If you can hold a pencil, you can draw. If you can stand or sit upright, you can dance.

4. *When I start doubting myself, I sometimes feel like giving up. No matter how many times I've given a speech, I'm afraid I'll forget my lines. No matter how many laughs my jokes have gotten, I'm afraid my comedy act is going to bomb. That's when I have to think of my 200-year timeline. I know in the long run, in 200 years or so, I'll have a positive effect on those around presently me. One day, one hour or one minute won't change that. So I can stop worrying.*

Most of the time, we worry about things that aren't going to happen. We play the "what if" game. What if my alarm clock doesn't work or what if the car doesn't start.

Worrying about something distracts you from preparing for it. And in most cases, the consequences aren't worth worrying about. If the alarm doesn't work and you miss your ride to the airport, you'll have to take another plane.

It might upset your plans, but 200 years from now no one will remember it.

5. *Almost no one becomes a success overnight. In fact, I may never get to the place I've imagined for myself. But I'm enjoying the process of trying to get there. If today is the best I'll ever be, I'm thankful for the cool stuff I have, the interesting places I've been and the amazing people I've met.*

I'm one of those guys who likes to shoot for the stars. I may be living in Tyner, Indiana, but I can imagine myself being a major success in the world's best comedy clubs. I would like to have my own TV show and to be in a movie.

Those things haven't happened yet. I'm still working on them.

While I'm shooting for the stars, I'm also aiming for the ground I'm on. I'm happy every day, wherever I am, whatever I'm doing, whomever I'm with.

It's not New York or Hollywood, but you'll never hear me complain about Tyner.

6. *People who believe in handicaps are constantly creating obstacles for themselves. They are allowing themselves to stop, to quit, to settle for less than they deserve. Everyone's life has difficult spots. Those are times you have a chance to grow and to learn new ways to do things.*

We all know people who seem to have perfect lives.

They've had good families, they went to good schools, have good jobs, have good marriages and seem to have no problems at all. Compared to them, our lives seem so small. But in fact, if there's one thing all humans share, it's the challenges. Even the happiest families face sorrow and setbacks.

At the very core, we all live with the knowledge that we're all going to die someday. You can let that cast a shadow over everything you do, or you can use that as motivation to make every day count.

Handicaps aren't just physical. For most people, they're emotional. We grow up with low self-esteem or problems with anger management or depression.

Our task as humans is to recognize our weaknesses, our handicaps, and figure out a way to overcome them. We find strengths within us to overcome our challenges.

Life may seem better for the people who are gently floating downstream. In reality, the fun is when you get knocked out of that boat and swim.

7. *I am better than no one, and no one is better than I. It's easy to feel intimidated when someone else uses their social or career status to put you down. For someone like me, people of all sorts feel superior, that they have something I can't get. You hear them say, "I feel so sorry for you." Forget that. No one is better than I am, and I am no better than they.*

As I've said earlier in the book, when I enter a business for the first time, I always want to meet the owner. I want them to know who I am and what I'm about. But I spend just as much energy getting to know the people who sweep the floors and clean the toilets.

I have much in common with people at both ends of the spectrum. I feel I have great wealth, maybe not in money, but in other ways. I also feel I have to work really hard at things, often without receiving much in return.

Anything you have can be taken away. I'm not just talking about worldly goods, either. If you feel superior to me because you have arms and legs while I don't, you need to recognize that your advantage is temporary. At any given moment, through an injury or illness, you could end up with less than I have.

If I have any advantage over you, maybe it's that I know that having no arms and legs isn't so bad.

8. *I like being different. It sets me apart and opens me up for more positive attention. But some folks are uncomfortable when they confront something new. One of the keys is to break the ice for people who may not be comfortable with you. Give them a reason to find out who you really are.*

I know people who will stay away from an event they really want to attend simply because they aren't looking their best. They'll let a bad hair day ruin their plans.

Get over it.

I've had a lifetime of getting strange looks. The best thing to do is to put a smile on your face and let people learn what a cool person you can be.

If someone notices your bad hair or your missing tooth, that's all they'll remember unless you give them a good reason. Say hello. Give them a smile.

9. *A good first impression is essential. People have all*

kinds of different ways of greeting each other. Some folks kiss. Some shake hands. Other nod or just say, "Wazzup." For me, I like a handshake. If I extend my arm, grab the end of it, just like you would someone's hand. If you meet someone new and don't know what to do, it's OK to ask. That gives us a chance to figure things out together.

No one knows awkward better than I do. For me, each first meeting requires a little extra attention. Most people find it hard to believe I want to shake their hand.

If you don't know what to do, ask. It's simple. "Are we shaking hands or hugging?" A smile or a laugh will get you through.

If you're feeling awkward about it, don't try to duck out. I mean, how much courage will I think you have if you're afraid of addressing me.

Don't make me chase after you to get my handshake.

10. "You're never stuck, you're just temporaily delayed."

11. Two of the most powerful words are "thank you." Too often, we're surprised by a sincere compliment and act like we don't deserve anyone's praise. When you say "thank you," you're telling the other person their words are appreciated and you're telling yourself that maybe they're right.

I know a lot of people who feel like they have to

say something clever in response to a compliment. More often than not, they end up getting their words all twisted up and might end up offending the other person.

Walk to the mirror right now, look yourself in the eye and say, "Thank you."

Isn't that easy?

12. *There's a fine line between laughing at your situation and making fun of yourself to receive negative attention. It's like a card game. Sometimes you're dealt a bad hand. If you enjoy the game, you don't mind losing once in a while. That's part of the joy of living. But if you tear yourself down when you lose, the game's no fun.*

Unless you're some sort of superstar, you're going to win about half the games you play and lose the other half. It's nice to win, but it's just as nice to lose if you respect the people you're competing with.

One thing I've noticed about losing is that it gives you a better chance to reveal the type of person you are. Some people feel they have to blame the referees, their opponents, the weather, their coaches or their fans. Others feel they should laugh it off, like they really weren't playing to win anyway.

Personally, after I whip someone at pool or darts or some other game, I want them to ask for a rematch. That gives me a chance to whip them again. Just kidding…talking smack. What I really mean is, that I like it when they show no fear in shame of losing and just enjoy playing.

13. *We are not here to judge others. You can't judge someone unless you know everything about them. And unless you can read minds, you'll never be able to do that. I believe there is a final judge for all of us. I'll let His decision stand.*

I run into a lot of people who act like jerks. Generally, if I spend enough time with them, I figure out some reason to like them.

When you're meeting someone for the first time, you never know if they've just had the worst day of their life. Give them a second chance or a third or a fourth. The larger the sample you get, the more likely you are to find the truth.

+++
+++

And now we're at the end of the book. Thank you for coming this far with me.

These are just some of the lessons I've learned so far. By the time the ink dries on the page, I hope to have learned more. I figure, when you stop learning, you stop living. And I'm much too young to stop either of those.

The best thing for me and for you is if we stay in touch somehow. That's a lot easier nowadays. You won't have to ride on a horse from India to Great Britain to catch up with me.

I have a web site. I have an email address.

I know a lot of the things I've learned have been through trial and error. I've tried a lot of things and fallen, literally, flat on my face.

One of the things I've found out is that there's a better way to learn. It's called sharing. Your experiences and ideas can help me avoid some of those mistakes.

That's why I'm asking you for the greatest gift of all: Let's stay in touch. You've heard from me. Now it's time for me to hear from you. Help me learn. When I know what you know, I truly can say that I'm not missing anything.

Thanks.